The
PENNY-PINCHING
PREPPER

D1557615

The
PENNY-PINCHING
PREPPER

SAVE MORE, SPEND LESS
AND GET PREPARED FOR ANY DISASTER

BERNIE CARR

Ulysses Press

Published in the US by:
Ulysses Press
P.O. Box 3440
Berkeley, CA 94703
www.ulyssespress.com

ISBN: 978-1-61243-487-2
Library of Congress Control Number: 2015937560

Printed in the United States by Bang Printing

10 9 8 7 6 5 4 3 2 1

Acquisitions editor: Keith Riegert
Managing editor: Claire Chun
Editor: Renee Rutledge
Proofreader: Lauren Harrison
Indexer: Sayre Van Young
Front cover design: Rebecca Lown
Interior design: what!design @ whatweb.com
Cover artwork: pistols © Orfeev/shutterstock.com, bushcraft icons © zelimirz/shutterstock.com, camping icons © Panptys/shutterstock.com, survival kit icon © supirloko89/shutterstock.com, penny © Pete Spiro/shutterstock.com
Layout: Lindsay Tamura
Illustrations: Evan Wondolowski

Distributed by Publishers Group West

CONTENTS

INTRODUCTION

I started my preparedness journey soon after Hurricane Ike in 2008. In the aftermath of the hurricane, many Houston communities were left without power for several days, roads were flooded, and food deliveries to numerous area stores were delayed. It was then that I learned that when the trucks stop coming, grocery stores quickly become emptied. I resolved to be prepared and have enough supplies to sustain my family for a few weeks in case of emergencies. I read everything I could get my hands on, online and at the library, about food storage, water purification, the best backpack to have, fire starting, emergency shelters, and all manner of gear. While living in the city, I chronicled my own family preparedness steps in my blog, *Apartment Prepper*. In 2010, I wrote *The Prepper's Pocket Guide*, a book about taking small, easy steps to prepare for disasters.

Over the years I have received hundreds of emails from readers who want to know how to find extra money to spend on being prepared. A common misconception, due in part to TV shows such as *Doomsday Preppers*, where many of the featured individuals appear to have an unlimited source of income to pour into their preparedness and survival supplies, is that you need to have a lot of money to be prepared. In "TV land" that may be the case, but out in the real world, most preppers are just ordinary folks with jobs struggling to make ends meet. I won't lie, there is some outlay, and certainly a lot of prioritizing involved, but it does not have to be out of reach for average people.

With all the interest in preparedness and improving one's finances, the idea to write *The Penny-Pinching Prepper* was born.

WHAT ARE YOU PREPARING FOR?

If you read any emergency preparedness books or survival blogs, there is always a list of perils to be ready for, ranging in severity from a simple snowstorm to more terrifying disasters such as nuclear war or an EMP (electromagnetic pulse) that takes down the power grid. Of course there are lots of other threats in between, including natural disasters, epidemics, or economic upheavals. And let's not forget personal disasters such as job loss, divorce, and medical disability. Just thinking about all these possibilities can become overwhelming, but don't let yourself get carried away.

The best way to approach this is to consider the most common threats in your immediate area. Some areas are prone to hurricanes, earthquakes, snowstorms, tornadoes, etc. While some people may fear a natural disaster, others may feel insecure in their employment situation and feel a job loss may be imminent. What are the most likely threats facing you?

Answer this question and you can start prioritizing your needs and plan your expenses.

The good news is, once you get started preparing for one thing, you will have a good foundation to be prepared for other types of disasters.

IS YOUR PARTNER ON BOARD WITH PREPARING?

This is another question you must ask. If you have not brought up the subject of being prepared with your significant other, now is the time to do so. The process of getting ready will be a lot easier if your partner shares your enthusiasm. Becoming a prepared household is a joint decision. If your partner does not share your desire to be prepared, try to understand his or her point of view. Sometimes people are resistant to being prepared because of fear or lack of understanding about the need to be prepared. Do not try to argue and be confrontational. Instead, approach the subject in terms of immediate regional threats, such as being prepared for earthquakes or hurricanes. Another good approach for parents is the idea of protecting the children and making sure they are safe in a disaster. Start slow and soon your partner will realize the benefits such as money savings from your stockpile as well as an increased feeling of security that comes from being prepared.

TIME- AND MONEY-SAVER

Since I started the journey to be more prepared, I have found lots of ways to save myself both time and money. By adopting a mindset of being ready, you will avoid lots of unnecessary expenses and wasted time. How is this possible? In the coming pages, you will find out.

HOW TO GET THE MOST OUT OF THIS BOOK

Chapter 1 of this book deals with saving money and finding extra funds that can be used for emergency preparation as well as building your cash cushion. In Chapter 2 and thereafter, I will give you lots of ideas on preparing for emergencies with a small budget. The fun part is being able to make some of your own preps with stuff you already have around the house.

You can start your preparedness journey AND save money simultaneously. You don't have to do this in any order. The only thing you need to do is just get started.

RAISING ADDITIONAL FUNDS FOR EMERGENCY SUPPLIES

This may sound like a cliché, but I have to say it anyway. A great first step to saving money and getting started with being prepared is to get organized. By taking this first step, you will get your finances in order and identify your important papers by eliminating all the junk.

ELIMINATE CLUTTER

You may be wondering why a penny pincher's preparedness guide would go over the exercise of getting organized. Clutter may seem harmless enough, but it ends up costing you money in the long run. For instance:

- Have you missed a credit card payment and gotten charged a late payment fee?

- Have you been charged an overdraft fee because you forgot to balance your checkbook for a couple of weeks and lost track of how much you had?

- How many times have you had to run to the mall and buy the first thing you spotted, at full price because you forgot someone's birthday was coming up?

- Do you have a huge stack of papers that you have not looked at or filed?

I have missed out on deals and allowed gift certificates to expire from being disorganized and burying these opportunities under piles of paper.

Getting organized applies to both paperwork and electronic records. Not long ago, I took my car for an oil change and ended up paying full price because I did not print the email offer for a 25 percent discount. It had gotten buried in my overly full inbox. I was really annoyed at myself and resolved not to let my inbox get that full again.

Knowing what to save and what to keep will also help you choose which files to grab in the event of an emergency. If you had to evacuate your home in a hurry, you would know exactly where birth certificates, home, car, and life insurance policies, passports, etc., are stored and will avoid wasting time looking for things.

Financial Records

Take a half day to sort through all your paperwork and throw out anything that is no longer necessary. Separate the piles into:

1. Action needed

2. To file

3. Throw out

- Go through your email inbox as well. Delete all emails that are too old.

- If an action is needed, do what needs to be done and get it over with. Then you can file or toss the paper or email.

- Get all your credit card statements together; we will go over them in the next step.

- Get all your monthly bills together, including car payment, rent or mortgage, utility bills, etc.

- If you have coupons or gift cards, set them in a pile where you can see them and resolve to start using them this week. Many small checks and refunds are only good for 30 to 45 days. Don't let them go to waste. Similarly, some gift cards have penalties: When unused for a certain amount of time their values start to dwindle.

- Cash those small checks and add the money to your emergency fund. You can use those department store gift cards to add to your emergency kit.

HOW LONG TO KEEP PAPERWORK

Utility Bills	1 year
Credit Card Statements	1 year
Tax Records	7 years
Sales Receipts	length of the return period, which is on the receipt itself
Tax-Deductible Receipts	7 years
Bank Statements	1 year
Birth Records	indefinitely
Marriage Certificate	indefinitely
Divorce Decree	indefinitely
Immunization Records	indefinitely
Mortgage Records	as long as you own your house
Proof of Auto Ownership	as long as you own your vehicle

WHAT TO KEEP AND WHAT TO TOSS

Utility bills and credit card statements: *One year.* These can accumulate quickly. Here's an organization tip: Use a three-ring binder and separate each month with tabs. For each month, add a plastic protector that has a sleeve where you can insert that month's paid bills. This is an easy way to keep a record of everything you paid. It is also your "go-to" source to check past bills and payments. Having the three-ring binder for statements has come in handy countless times when I've found questionable charges and errors. All you have to do is review previous months' records and you can make an easy comparison.

Tax records: *Seven years.*

Receipts: *Three months to seven years.* I keep receipts in case I have to return a purchase. Only keep them during the return period, such as 3 months. Bank receipts for deposits should be kept until you see the item properly recorded in your online or paper statement. However, receipts for items that you deducted from taxes, such as those from charitable contributions, should be kept for seven years.

Bank statements: *One year.*

Items to keep indefinitely: Birth records, marriage certificate, divorce decree, immunization records, mortgage records (as long as you own your house), proof of auto ownership.

Free Up Space for Supplies

You will need to allocate some space for emergency supplies, especially if you live in a small space.

Set aside 15 to 30 minutes a day to go through all the rooms and closets in your home and find items you have not used in a year. I don't mean seasonal items such as Christmas or other holiday decorations or seasonal clothes; I mean old stuff you are keeping around "just in case." These include:

- clothes that no longer fit, have never fit, and probably never will
- items you keep due to guilt
- multiple versions of one item that you will never use

- gifts once given to you or your family that no one likes
- crafting projects you've kept but never finished
- furniture or appliances that are never used

The High Cost of Clutter

Hanging on to too many items can be a pitfall even for frugal people. Many people have so much stuff they pay for storage units for many years. Most storage units contain old furniture, outdated appliances, and old clothes. Over the years, paying the storage facility a monthly fee may end up costing more than the items themselves are worth.

People hang on to things just in case they might need them later, but they end up misplacing or losing track of most of it. Clutter also fools you into thinking you have something that in reality you don't. When the time comes that you need a particular item, you will end up buying a new one if you cannot find the original buried in your junk. I should know, as this happened to me before I changed my habits.

You need to make room for your emergency supplies. Getting rid of junk will ensure that you will have room for your food storage and emergency gear. As you go through each area of your living space, separate the piles of unneeded or unwanted items into the following:

Gift items. Give these to someone who can use them. Some family members may appreciate the hand-me-downs, and they, in turn, will return the favor someday. We have a system in our family, where the oldest cousins pass their used clothes and toys to the younger cousins, who then keep passing them down. Kids outgrow clothes so quickly—clothes don't get worn often enough to wear out.

Donations. Donate the item to charity and get a receipt for your taxes.

Stuff you can sell. Sell the items in a garage sale, via eBay, or through Craigslist. To ensure your safety, meet your potential buyer in a public place, such as a fast-food restaurant or in front of a bank, fire station, or police station. Keep a private list of your items' serial numbers. Never arrange a meeting in your home. Later in the book, we will go further into these methods of making extra cash.

Junk. If broken or unusable, just throw the item in the trash.

HOW TO HAVE A SUCCESSFUL GARAGE SALE

1. Make sure your homeowner's association or apartment lease allows garage sales. Some towns require permits, so check on requirements before you schedule one. You should also check on regulations regarding the posting of garage sale signs. You wouldn't want to end up with a ticket for posting in a restricted area.

2. Partner up with another family or two, especially if they are experienced with garage sales. With a wider variety of inventory, you'll attract more buyers. Agree on how to split the profits in advance.

3. Advertise. Craigslist and neighborhood garage sale sites on Facebook are free.

4. Thoroughly examine all the items you are planning to sell: Check pockets, boxes, pots and pans, pull-out drawers, etc., to make sure you did not leave anything inside that you did not intend to sell.

5. Organize your items well. Place larger-ticket items in front. Put price stickers on each item, but don't set the prices too high. You want to sell these items off, not hold on to them.

6. Be prepared to haggle.

7. Keep your dog on a leash or inside the house.

8. Set up early in the morning. You may schedule the garage sale to start at 9 a.m., but the early birds may start showing up at 7 a.m. You might as well be ready.

9. Once you are all set up and ready, place eye-catching signs in well-traveled intersections, with good directions. Use neon poster boards or balloons to attract attention.

10. Have plenty of change. You should have various denominations, especially $1 bills and rolls of quarters, dimes, nickels, and pennies. Keep your money in a safe place, such as a fanny pack.

11. Make sure someone is staffing the garage sale at all times. Watch out for shoplifters.

12. Post "All Sales Are Final." You don't want any returns a few days later.

13. Have a box labeled "Freebies." It attracts more customers.

14. Don't forget packaging. Have a lot of plastic grocery bags available for buyers, as well as old newspaper to wrap up breakable items.

15. Donate unsold items as soon as the sale is over.

REDUCE DEBT

A lot of people ask this question: Can you prep if you are deep in debt? Sure you can! Being in debt is a heavy burden but it does not mean you should not prepare for emergencies. In fact, getting into a preparedness mindset will help you avoid a lot of predicaments that lead to debt, such as missing payment deadlines, forgetting to pay your car insurance, or ignoring needed car repairs.

What you should not do is get into more debt by buying a lot of gear all at once. Now let's look at what you can do to reduce or eliminate debt.

Credit Cards

SHOULD YOU STOP USING THEM?

Just take them out of your wallet or purse and store them away in a safe, out of the premises if you have a safe deposit box.

Or place them in a container of water to keep in your freezer. Having a credit card handy all the time is very tempting. Years ago, before I learned these hard lessons, I got into credit card debt and it was bad enough to keep me up at night. Those minimum monthly payments can add up. Pretty soon all the payments that seemed so small before add up until you no longer have money for rent, food, and gas. The situation can quickly escalate into a full-blown financial emergency with collection agents calling, your car being repossessed, and eviction. Don't let credit card debt swallow you up in a downward spiral. Stop using the cards now. I'm not saying credit cards are evil and you should stay away from them forever. We need to just put them away to avoid temptation.

SHOULD YOU CANCEL A CREDIT CARD?

Some sites recommend canceling credit cards altogether and say you should never use them. I disagree with this advice because canceling a card may negatively affect your credit score, especially if you still have a balance. Your credit report will show the card's final balance and without any remaining credit on the card, it will appear to be maxed out. When you pay off the balance, you can choose to cancel it, but again, if you do not have credit, it will negatively affect your score. I have a friend who paid off all his cards, canceled some of them, and never touched credit for two years. When he checked his credit score before buying a car, he found that it had gone down even lower than it was before. He spoke with a banker and was told that because he no longer used credit, it appeared he did not have a good history of paying month after month. A good financial history shows you are paying your obligations on time every month. To build back his credit, he charged small amounts, up to $100 or so, and made regular payments to show he always paid on time.

WHY YOU NEED GOOD CREDIT

Having good credit is necessary these days: It helps determine the rates you will be charged for home, auto, and other loans. Credit is also reviewed for rental applications, and potential employers check credit ratings for applicants, especially if the position involves access to money. Auto and home insurers also check credit when issuing new policies.

SNOWBALL METHOD

Remember the credit card statements we collected in the "What to Keep and What to Toss" section? Now we will look at those statements and have a reality check. On a piece of paper or spreadsheet, make columns for amount owed, minimum monthly payment, interest rate, and date due. List the debts in order: Write down the one that has the lowest balance first, the second lowest next, and so on. Add up the totals of the debts and the minimum monthly payments.

I am a big believer in the "snowball method" of paying off debts. This method involves adding any extra amounts you can toward paying off the card with the smallest balance, while paying the minimums on all others. I know that applying the extra payment to the one with the highest interest is more prudent, but psychologically, it will be a huge "win" for you to pay off the one with the lowest balance at the fastest possible time.

Here is an example of how it works:

Debt	Amount Owed	Interest Rate	Minimum Monthly Payment	Extra Payment	Total Payment
Credit Card A	$900	8%	$50	$10	$60
Credit Card B	$1,500	10%	$75	$0	$75
Credit Card C	$2,000	12%	$100	$0	$100
Credit Card D	$4,500	9%	$225	$0	$225

If you have extra money you can apply to the payments, even if it is $10 per month, apply it to Card A, the one with the lowest balance.

Once you have paid off Card A, take the amount you were paying them and add it to the amount you are paying Card B, the next card with the lowest balance.

Even if you don't pay any extra, you will still end up paying Card A off first, in which case you can then add the amount you were paying Card A to Card B. Now that you are paying extra to Card B, the "snowball" gets larger, allowing you to pay it off faster.

The key to making this debt repayment plan work is not charging additional amounts to any of the cards.

LOWER YOUR MONTHLY BILLS

You may think there is nothing more you can do about your bills and therefore consider them fixed amounts.

Go through your check register and list all your monthly bills. Include:

- rent or mortgage
- electricity
- natural gas
- water and sewer
- cell phone
- cable and internet
- magazine subscriptions
- gym membership
- bank fees

Make a note of what you have been paying each month and resolve to lower your expenditures.

If your checking account incurs a monthly fee, find another bank or account that does not. Most of the time, banks will not charge monthly fees for accounts that have direct deposit.

Before you switch banks, do some research on incentives for opening a new account. Banks are very competitive these days, so take advantage of any offers that you get in the mail. Some banks and credit unions offer $50 to $100 for opening a new account. Read the fine print. They usually indicate they will pay after 1 to 3 months from the date the account was opened. Mark your calendar where you expect the bonus to occur. Sometimes, the bank neglects to give you the credit until you remind them. Recently, a new credit union opened up close to my office and they offered $25 for a "youth account," so I took my son to open a new savings account. After the allotted time, I noticed the account had not received the $25 credit, but a quick call to the credit union manager rectified the oversight.

Review your checking accounts and credit card statements and check for any errors. Not too long ago, I discovered some unfamiliar charges in my bank statement. One was for $24.99, the others were for small amounts like $3.34, $9.99, etc. I found no one in the family had made any of these charges and they were fraudulent. I immediately reported the situation to my bank and they researched it. The bank's security department indicated that fraudulent charges are made in small amounts as crooks figure that most people do not check their accounts line by line and the small charges will not be noticed. The bank reissued our debit cards. After a couple of weeks, the bank agreed to refund the amounts to my account.

INSTANT MONEY TIP

Take advantage of new account offers from banks and credit unions and save on bank fees.

Electricity and Gas

Contact your power company and ask for an energy audit. Most companies will do an energy audit for free and the audit includes money saving tips.

Vampire Appliances

When you leave the house, unplug vampire appliances to save on power. These appliances are constantly using power, even when turned off: HDTVs, DVD players, video game consoles, microwave ovens, or any appliance that constantly has a light or a clock on. Many people leave their computers on, thinking the monitors will go on "sleep mode." Even a cell phone charger that is left plugged in the wall socket uses up energy.

Air Conditioning

Make sure all your vents are open. I used to think closing a vent saves on energy, but actually, a closed vent makes the air conditioner work harder, thereby using more energy.

Install a programmable thermostat.

Replace your air filter. The filter traps dust, pollen, pet hair, and dander. The dirtier the filter, the harder your A/C unit has to work and the more energy you use. Check and replace your air filter at least on a quarterly basis.

During comfortable days, open the windows instead of running the air conditioner. Since we live in a hot, humid area for most of the year, we keep the windows closed to save energy while cooling the house. But as soon as fall weather comes, we turn off the air conditioner and open the windows to let in the breeze.

Laundry Room

Use cold water when washing clothes. Using hot or warm water uses a lot more electricity, but does not improve the soil-fighting power. I think using hot water is harder on clothes and wears them out faster.

Do not overfill your clothes dryer as this also restricts air flow, making the dryer work harder and use more energy.

Do you have space to air dry clothes? By hanging clothes on a clothesline or even on hangers in the bathroom, you will save more energy.

Kitchen

Choose the appropriate-sized burner for the pot you are using. If you are using a small pot, do not use the large burner, as this wastes the heat. If your pot is large, using the small burner will take too long to heat the contents, requiring more energy.

Turn off the oven 5 minutes before the stated time in the recipe. The heat in the oven will be enough to continue cooking for those last minutes.

Refrigerator

Wait for hot foods to cool down before placing them in your fridge. The heat from the food will warm up the rest of your fridge and it will take more energy to cool it off again.

Don't overcrowd your refrigerator. If the airflow is restricted, the refrigerator uses more energy.

On the other hand, a full freezer is more efficient because all the frozen items allow new items to freeze more quickly.

TAP WATER VERSUS BOTTLED WATER

Except for travel and emergency water storage, I have stopped using bottled water in our household. The Environmental Protection Agency (EPA) actually has stricter requirements on tap water than the Food and Drug Administration (FDA) has on bottled water.

The bottled water industry would have you believe that bottled water is better in quality than tap, but in reality, the difference is usually due to taste, not overall water safety.

Here are a few ways to improve the taste of tap water:

- Run tap water through a home water filter. I will cover water filters more extensively in Chapter 2.
- Store your drinking water in a glass container instead of a plastic one. Let it stand for a few hours before drinking.
- Chill water before drinking.
- Add a squeeze of lemon or lime to your drinking water.

Invest in a few reusable containers (one for each member of the family) and you will save a few hundred dollars previously used to buy bottled water.

Water

Use your dishwasher's "quick wash" setting. Don't overcrowd the dishes or they will not be washed properly and you will end up handwashing or repeating the cycle.

Take shorter showers.

Place a filled soda bottle in the corner of the toilet tank to displace some of the water needed to fill it.

Check for leaks. If your lawn has a constantly wet spot or if you see water flowing into the gutter and no one has the sprinkler turned on, chances are you have a leak.

Cell Phone

Read your bill and understand your charges. If the bill looks too complicated, call the customer service line and have them explain it to you line by line. I have done this and found the reps to be helpful.

Know when your contract is up and comparison shop between carriers.

Ask a customer service rep for ways to lower your bill. They can look at your usage patterns and identify if your usage is below your current plan allowances. For example, I was paying for an unlimited data plan but found my family's usage was less than 2 gigabytes a month. I lowered the bill by switching to a lower data plan. Just make sure that making changes will not extend your contract or penalize you in any way.

Cable and Internet

Similar to the cell phone, you will need to call the cable company and ask them to explain your bill.

Ask the rep how much time you have left in the contract. Even if you are on a contract, you can request to have a lower-cost plan and stay with the same company. Double check with your cable provider, but most contracts allow movement between plans, as long as you don't cancel completely.

If your contract has ended, comparison shop between providers. Call customer service and explain that you are trying to lower your bills because finances are tight. If you have done your homework, mention than another company is offering a special discounted rate. Most companies have a "Retention Department" that will offer you a special rate to keep your business.

Tip: Always ask a lot of questions and write everything down, including the names of everyone you talk to. Ask them to verify what was said before you hang up. Make sure you check your next bill so see that everything agreed upon is reflected correctly.

HOW TO GET RID OF CABLE AND SAVE EVEN MORE MONEY

Most cable packages increase in price after your initial introductory period has ended. Review the new charges carefully and decide if you are willing to pay a higher amount.

If you are no longer on contract, consider cutting the cable service altogether. I was able to cancel the services and still catch most of the shows the family likes by replacing it with lower-cost services. Here are some options:

- TV antenna or indoor HDTV antenna. A standard TV antenna costs around $12, and an indoor HDTV antenna costs around $60. You get all the regular network channels, but no cable channels. Monthly cost: $0

- Online programming. Most networks air recent episodes online, allowing you to catch the shows the next day or within a week of airing. Monthly cost: $0

- Roku 3. The Roku 3 is a device that connects to your TV and allows you to stream music, videos, shows, games, and other content from the Internet into your TV. The cost of the device is approximately $89. Monthly cost: Depends on which services you subscribe to.

- Netflix, Hulu, Amazon Prime. These services can be accessed directly from most newer TVs. They offer movies and many TV shows. Monthly cost: Prices vary.

At this time, Amazon Prime is $120 per year, but it also includes free priority mail shipping with your Amazon orders. Netflix and Hulu cost around $9 and up, depending on the services you subscribe to.

I have not had cable service for around 8 months now, and I can say I do not miss it at all. It takes a bit of research at first while trying to find services that fit your entertainment preferences, but the cost savings is substantial and therefore worth considering.

SAVING MONEY ON HEALTH CARE

Health Insurance Premiums

Each year, employers hold an open enrollment period when employees have an opportunity to choose their benefit package for the coming year. Don't ignore or rush through the information given during open enrollment. This may be the only chance you get to take advantage of benefits offered, unless you experience a "qualifying event" to switch plans, such as marriage, divorce or annulment, death, the birth or adoption of a child, new employment or termination of a spouse's, change in full-time or part-time status, etc.

Compare plans carefully, taking into account your health and usage patterns. If you have access to a Flexible Spending Account (FSA) or Health Savings Account (HSA), don't forget to use it to pay for your qualified medical expenses.

An FSA is a benefit offered by some employers in which pre-tax dollars are set aside by employees for health care and medical expenses such as prescription co-pays, eyeglasses, braces, etc. This lowers your taxable income on the upside, but since these plans have a "use it or lose it" rule, you will want to check your balance on a regular basis throughout the year and make sure you use all the funds that you contributed to before the end of the year.

HSAs are accounts set aside specifically for medical expenses, but can be carried over from year to year.

Preventive Care

Many health insurance plans cover preventive care at 100 percent coverage or very little out-of-pocket outlay.

Part of being prepared means staying healthy and being up to date on all your needed health checkups, age-related screenings, vaccinations, etc. For example, when was the last time you got your eyes checked? Have you had a tetanus shot in the last 10 years? Many adults are conscientious about getting their kids checked but neglect themselves until it is too late. Don't put off needed checkups and procedures.

Tip: Ask for pricing before receiving non-emergency care. Find out what is covered by insurance and what you will be responsible for. If you are able to, shop around before deciding.

A couple of years ago, my son needed his wisdom teeth extracted. Before choosing a dental surgeon, I called at least three providers in the area and compared rates. There was a big difference in the out-of-pocket costs. We also checked ratings and patient comments before proceeding. We ultimately chose the provider with a mid-priced quote and the highest ratings.

Choose wisely. Check your physicians' and dentist's licenses online by visiting your state's licensing board. Most states have a site where you type in the name and city and you will find out information such as schools attended, graduation year, years they have been licensed in your state, violations, and any malpractice suits.

Why go through all this trouble? Staying healthy is an important part of being prepared. Things can be so much worse if a disaster hits and your health fails you. At the same time, maintaining good health will save you money in the long-run.

Doctor visits. Before going on a non-emergency doctor visit, make sure you know what your insurance plan covers. For example, many doctors' offices automatically collect a co-pay, even though your plan may cover 100 percent of the cost of preventive care visits. Some offices may still insist on collecting up front, but as soon as you receive your insurance company's "Explanation of Benefits" (EOB) that shows the patient's responsibility portion of the bill, compare it against what the office charged you. You may be eligible for a refund. This has happened to me a few times. The easiest way to handle it is to make a call to the billing manager of the doctor's office. Explain that you paid up front but your insurance shows a lesser amount than what you paid. They will usually write you a check after they get their payment from your health insurance company.

Prescriptions. Ask for the generic versions of prescriptions when possible.

Speak with your physician about your budgetary concerns. Oftentimes, your doctor may know about money-saving offers or discount programs available from drug manufacturers. They may also have samples.

Shop around at various pharmacies for the best price.

Consider mail order or bulk sources. Many insurance companies have their own mail order drug providers.

COMBINING RESOURCES

If you combine resources with friends or family, you will be able to save some money.

Let's say you are close with a family, but you're unsure if they're as interested in preparing for emergencies as you are. How should you bring up the subject of preparedness? If you are shy about the topic and worried your friend might jump to conclusions about you, the best way to bring it up would be in passing, and not be intense or threatening about it. Here are some examples:

- Watch a movie or a TV show that involves a disaster, such as *The Day After Tomorrow*, *Independence Day*, or even a zombie flick. Ask, "What would you do if something like this were to happen?" A natural discussion would ensue and you will learn how they feel about being prepared. You may be pleasantly surprised.

- If you are closely related, a conversation during the beginning of the school year could revolve around emergency contacts and authorized emergency pickups. Every school needs backup contacts. Discuss each families' plans in case of an emergency during a school day and see where the conversation takes you.

You can tell a lot about a person by what their fridge contains. You'll get an idea how they feel about preparedness by seeing what kinds of food they stock up on and whether they have anything in the refrigerator at any given time. I have relatives who tend to have nothing in the fridge except for a jug of orange juice and maybe a yogurt. If they eat out every night, it is not likely they would be too concerned about emergencies.

But, if you do find a like-minded friend or family, you can then take the next step and start exchanging plans and potentially combining resources should an emergency happen:

- Be each other's emergency contact.
- Share a storage facility for supplies.
- Plan an escape route out of the city, should an emergency arise and it is no longer safe to stay in place. You can either leave together or meet up at a pre-arranged location.
- Buy bulk foods and medicines from a warehouse store and split the cost and quantities.
- Share in the cost of a piece of land for bugging out.
- Share equipment and tools. This would entail being conscientious about returning items to the proper owners and being gracious about lending as well.
- Take inventory of everyone's survival skills.

ALTERNATIVE INVESTMENTS

Many preppers wonder whether they should purchase alternative investments such as land and precious metals. Before making these long-term investments, make sure you are sufficiently prepared for emergencies with water, food, supplies, emergency cash, and minimal debt.

If you feel you have covered the basics and you have the discretionary funds, then the time may be right for you to look into buying precious metals and land.

Buying Vacant Land

What are you going to use the land for? Are you looking for a bug-out location, retirement site, vacation home, or hunting cabin? There are some important considerations to look at beforehand:

- Does the land have a water source?
- What is the proximity to large cities and developed areas?
- Are there utilities such as electricity and gas available in the area? How much clearing would you have to do? Is there room to plant a garden?
- What are the water and mineral rights associated with the property?
- What is the size of the lot?

- How much would you have to pay for property taxes?
- How close are you to the neighbors?
- How remote is the property? If the property is very remote, it may be difficult to transport building materials once you are ready to build a cabin, home, or barn.
- What type of wildlife and game are available in the property?
- Are there easements?
- How close is the property to the road?
- Is the property fenced or will you have to build one?
- What's the topography of the property, including elevation, trails, and other landmarks? For instance, is the land in a flood plain?

Few people have the large amount of cash needed to pay in full. If you need to finance the purchase of vacant land, you will need to search for a "land loan," usually provided by banks and credit unions in the area. Many lenders do not provide land loans as they are considered more risky than home mortgage loans. Or, the lender may require 50 percent down, which is a lot more than the 10 to 20 percent required to buy a home. Another variation may be a shorter loan term, such as a 10- or 15-year loan, and the interest would higher than the going rates for a mortgage loan.

Buying land can be expensive, but there are ways to search for lower-priced options or better terms.

OWNER-FINANCED

When you speak with the agent representing the owner, find out whether owner financing is available. If the owner is willing to finance, you will avoid having to deal with a bank and having the purchase appear in your credit report. You can also negotiate, through your agent, the purchase price, loan term, interest rate, and down payment. However, terms such as interest rate may vary widely, so do some research on the going rates in the area before you agree to anything.

BUYING LAND IN A TAX LIEN SALE

Every year, a percentage of land owners and/or homeowners fail to pay property taxes. When that happens, the county seizes the property and conducts a tax lien sale. Each state varies on the amount of time or waiting period a county tax collector has to file for a tax lien sale.

When the property comes up for sale, the county usually holds an auction. Again, the process may vary by state, but generally, the county will accept the property from the highest bidder, who then gets to place a lien on the property.

The owner then has an allotted time (e.g., one year) to repay the property taxes owed, plus interest. If you had won the bid in the auction and you paid the property taxes, you stand to get your money back plus interest from the owner.

However, if the owner fails to pay within the time frame allowed, you can then file a lawsuit to seek title to the property.

- Do some research on properties that are past due on real estate taxes.

- Get familiar with the property tax laws in the state.

- Do a physical check on the property so you know exactly what is in the property before you bid.

- Conduct a title search to see if anyone other than the current owner has ownership rights or liens against the property.

- Know all the deadlines involved. If the county has a long redemption period, say 2 to 3 years, you may need to pay additional property taxes for subsequent years.

Gaining ownership to a tax-distressed property requires patience and a lot of research but may be a viable option for those seeking to buy a property at a lower rate.

Precious Metals

When considering an investment in precious metals, gold or silver usually come to mind. Why? Gold has long been the currency of choice throughout past civilizations, and many countries today still own significant gold reserves.

Thus, owning gold is often a prepper's "safe investment." On the other hand, one can say, "You can't eat gold," which brings us back to the idea that you should have all your basic emergency supplies such as water, food, shelter, first aid, and defense taken care of before considering an investment in gold.

You should also consider that while it is a tangible investment, the price of gold can swing wildly, with current spot prices hovering around $1,186 per ounce as of this writing, down from highs in the $1,500s a few years ago. The old adage "Buy low, sell high" may apply here, and many will consider buying a few gold coins when the price is right for them.

If you do decide to add gold and silver to your investments, here are some considerations:

- Always buy from a reputable dealer. Visit a gold dealer who is highly recommended by someone with whom you do business. Rare coin dealers, jewelers, and dental laboratories all have access to gold and may be willing to buy or sell gold on your behalf. Before making any deals or purchases, do a search online and check their ratings with the Better Business Bureau.

- Know what you are buying. You should make sure you are buying actual coins or bars, instead of a promissory note or investor certificates. I have seen many late-night commercials for "authentic gold coins" that are nothing more than worthless metal coins with a thin veneer of gold-plated coating.

- Always check values before buying and selling. A good source for checking gold and silver values online is Coinflation.com.

- Gold is more valuable than silver. One ounce of gold is worth a lot more than an ounce of silver. As mentioned, gold is at $1,186 per ounce at this time, while silver is running at about $17.07 per ounce. So if you are concerned about portability and storing the most value at the least weight, gold would be your choice.

- On the other hand, silver is more affordable and also offers more flexibility should you ever have to spend it. How would you spend an ounce of gold without having to physically cut it into pieces? Because silver comes in many denominations, including small amounts like quarters and nickels, it would be a lot easier to spend it on necessities.

A LOW-COST WAY TO ACQUIRE SILVER

Prior to 1965, United States coins contained 90 percent silver. Therefore, if you can acquire half dollars, quarters, and dimes from this time period you would own coins that have a high silver content. In addition, Kennedy half dollars minted from 1965 to 1969 contain 40 percent silver and are also desirable to own. You can purchase these high-silver-content coins from coin dealers and even auction sites such as eBay. Always research the seller and check ratings thoroughly before buying.

YOUR SUPPLIES AS AN INVESTMENT

A well-stocked pantry with several months' worth of consumable commodities is an investment in itself. If you buy rice, beans, sugar, salt, and flour in bulk now, chances are these same items will cost more next year. By buying these necessities before prices rise, you are ensuring that food will be available for your family should things become scarce. At the same time, you are instantly saving on cost, since the food you bought was purchased at a much cheaper price.

TURN HOBBIES INTO INCOME GENERATORS

A great way to generate extra money is with your hobbies or skills.

1. If you are crafty, sell your creations on Etsy at craft fairs, or at flea markets.

2. Do you like pets? I know a lady at work who pet sits for people when they go on vacation. She gets to stay in nice homes for the weekend as she watches over the owner's dogs and cats. Walking dogs is another way to put your animal-loving skills to use.

3. Start a blog or website about your favorite hobby. Once you have enough readers following your site, you can generate income by selling ad space.

4. Get paid to write articles as a freelancer.

5. Sell your photographs online.

6. Are you great at cleaning? You can clean houses on the weekends. A couple of ladies in my building charge $80 for 4 hours of work.

7. Are you an expert at organization? Lots of people don't know where to start when it comes to clearing out clutter. Hire yourself out as a professional organizer. I have one coworker who paid a consultant a few hundred dollars to help her decide what to keep and what to throw out when she sold her house.

8. If you can sew, you have a valuable skill. Lots of people would pay money to have their pants hemmed pants or for other minor alterations. Start with your own neighborhood; there won't be a shortage of customers.

9. Do you have a green thumb? Sell your plants at flea markets or farmer's markets.

10. If everyone consults you about ideas for throwing great parties, you could be a part-time party planner.

11. Like shopping? You could be a part-time personal shopper or work as a mystery shopper for companies.

It may take a small investment in time, but if you enjoy your activity and would do it for free anyway, it would be worthwhile for you to consider making extra money on the side.

BARTERING

Bartering is a great way to get what you need, without spending money.

You can barter items or services with others who have similar interests and needs. For example, you can organize a clothing swap with your coworker or neighbors, or set up a system of hand-me-downs with relatives and friends. You can also organize a toy swap with other parents whose children are close in ages. Or, you can barter services instead, such as haircuts, pet grooming or walking, babysitting, house cleaning, tax preparation, computer repair, and medical or dental services. There is really no limit to what you can barter. To avoid issues, agree on all the details in advance, such as the items or services being exchanged, time frame when the service or swap is to be done, and what each party considers a fair trade.

THE CASH EMERGENCY FUND

Most people think of being prepared in terms of having water, food, medicines, and other supplies on hand in case of an emergency. However, there is one other crucial item you will need, especially for everyday emergencies: the emergency cash fund.

There are hundreds of small emergencies that can happen, requiring you to have some cash on hand: You can lose your debit or credit cards, or identity theft or a bank glitch can cause you to lose access to your accounts. Or, an extended power outage could result in ATMs simply not working. It only makes sense to have a small amount of emergency cash tucked away in the car and at home for such emergencies. It can be as little as $20 in the glove compartment in case you need gas money or a few hundred dollars in a hidden spot in your home.

Here are some ways to generate cash and increase your emergency fund:

- Remember all the decluttering you did in the beginning of this chapter? Collect these items from all over your home and hold a garage sale. You could generate a few hundred dollars in one weekend.

- Don't spend all the gift money you receive on birthdays and holidays. Instead, save that money for your emergency stash.

- Sell unwanted gift cards online at sites such as GiftCardGranny.com (and other similar sites).

- Send in rebate forms for products you already use and save the cash received.

- Use coupons at the grocery store and instead of applying them to your balance, pay the amount in full and save the coupon money.

- Pick up change you find on the street and store it in a jar. At the end of the year you may have a few dollars' worth.

- Sell your unwanted books, DVDs, and electronics online.

The "No-Spend" Week

For a nice infusion of cash for your emergency fund, hold a "No-Spend Week" in your household. Agree with family members that you will only spend for gas to get to work that week. This means no eating out or shopping for groceries, clothes, or makeup. Agree to use whatever you have in your pantry and closets for that week. Use the recipes in this book for making cleaners, detergents, and personal care products using ingredients you already have at home.

The only exception would be for prescription medicines. It may be tough at first and it will take a bit of planning, but at the end of the week you should have saved a few hundred dollars.

Chapter 2

WATER

There was one time in my life when I truly realized the great need for water. Years ago, my family and I went hiking in the mountains for the very first time. After carefully studying the maps and researching the area, we calculated how much water we would carry in our packs to last until we got to our intended destination. Since this was our first time, we did not realize how long it would actually take to get to the lake camp with kids and dogs. We had already been hiking for 6 hours through very steep trails and switchbacks. The lake was nowhere in sight and it was getting dark. Although the temperature was mild, in the high seventies, the exertion of walking and carrying our packs required a lot more water than we had calculated. We were running out of water quickly and started to ration it for the kids. There was only enough water to take very small sips. We made camp in the dark without having reached the lake and spent one thirsty, miserable night. This was the first time I experienced real thirst—my throat was so parched it was hard to sleep. The next day, we continued the hike and eventually got to an area where we could procure water.

A person can survive around 3 weeks without food but only around 3 days without water. We endured one night of thirst and that was enough. I will never forget the dry, parched feeling in my mouth and throat when I could think of nothing else. From then on, I resolved that water would always be on the top of my list, whether planning a trip or preparing for emergencies.

Water is critical for survival and that is why we will address water storage and purification even before discussing food.

STORING WATER

How much water do you need to store? You need water not only for drinking but for cooking, washing, and cleaning. You also need water for your pets. The rule of thumb is to store a minimum of 1 gallon per person, per day, for however many days you want to cover. At the very least, you should have 7 to 10 days' worth of water stored within easy access. If you have the space and means to store more, then that is even better.

Free or Nearly Free

Reused food-grade bottles. The fastest way to get started is by reusing empty bottles of products you already buy, such as 2-liter soda bottles, juice bottles, or even wine bottles. Two 2-liter soda bottles amount to roughly a gallon of water.

DOES BOTTLED WATER EXPIRE?

According to the FDA, bottled water has an indefinite shelf life if the water is produced according to their quality standards and stored in an unopened, well-sealed container. They do not actually require expiration dates for bottled water but allow bottling companies to place expiration dates for their own use.

Bottled water may develop an off odor and taste when stored long-term. Store bottled water away from any chemical products that give off fumes that will permeate and spoil your water's quality and taste. In an emergency, you can use expired bottled water, but run it through a filter if you want to improve the taste.

I do not recommend milk jugs because milk fats and proteins stay in the plastic even after washing. For this reason, milk jugs encourage bacterial growth and tend to smell bad after a while.

Wash your soda and juice bottles thoroughly with soap and water. Rinse well until no soap bubbles appear. Using a dropper, add 2 to 3 drops of unscented, plain household bleach and some water and rinse again.

Fill them with tap water. Add 2 drops of the same unscented household bleach to prevent moss from growing. Seal the cap tightly. Store in a cool, dark place, away from any other containers that give out fumes. Ideally, you should rotate the water every 6 months. Or, use and replace the bottles before the year is up. Don't forget to replace the water as you use it up.

Food-grade buckets. You can also store water in food-grade 5-gallon buckets which can be obtained inexpensively or for free. Many bakeries and restaurants discard 5-gallon buckets that contained food ingredients or sauces used for baking or cooking. Since they are already food-grade, all you have to do is wash them thoroughly and they are ready to use.

Quick but More Expensive

If you feel an urgent need to prepare but don't want to wait until you have collected reusable bottles, buy generic bottled water when it goes on sale. Buy enough to cover about a week's worth for drinking. The advantage of having water bottles on hand is that they are portable.

Moderately Priced

To increase your water storage capacity, you can also purchase additional containers. One such inexpensive container is the WaterBOB, a plastic containment system that fits in a standard tub. It holds around 100 gallons of water and is made of heavy-duty plastic material that is food-grade and BPA free. The key would be to fill it up with water well before a foreseeable emergency, such as a hurricane or ice storm. If you wait too long, there may not be any water available.

Why do you need a liner—why not just fill up the tub? Well, I have considered this as well, and there may be a few reasons why it is not advisable to fill the tub with drinking water. First, materials used for constructing tubs were not meant for contact with drinking water. There may be contaminants that could leach into the water from the porcelain and caulking. Second, tubs get grimy, and not everyone cleans their tub on a daily basis. Finally, even if you do clean your tub, you were likely to have used harsh cleaners, which again, would not make it safe for drinking. However, if all you use the water for is washing, it would be fine, but you might as well use a liner if you can so the water would be safe for drinking as well.

Stackable water bricks. Water bricks that stack up vertically have recently become available. These are ideal for those who are short on space. Each brick holds 3.5 gallons; you can expand your storage by adding more containers.

Rain barrels. Rain barrels can hold around 50 to 55 gallons or more. They are stored outside to collect rainwater.

You would need a downspout from a gutter to feed into the barrel, as well as space to store it. The water can be used for washing, or if used for drinking, must be filtered and purified.

You can try to obtain a plastic rain barrel for free, but you would need to make sure the previous contents were non-toxic. Some possible sources might be bottling companies or food/soda manufacturers. If you were to purchase one, they run at about $35 and up from home and garden or discount stores.

EMERGENCY WATER SOURCES

Water heater. Your home's water heater is a good source of clean, drinkable water. An average home or apartment's water heater contains at least 30 gallons of clean water. Before an emergency happens, take the time to learn where your water heater is located and read the instructions (usually posted on the water heater) on how to drain the water.

Your refrigerator and freezer. In the event of power going out during an emergency, use up perishable drinks first. Most refrigerators contain milk and fruit juices that will spoil if not kept cold.

Tip: Fill your freezer with soda bottles containing drinking water. Leave enough room on top for expansion. In an emergency you can melt the ice and use for drinking.

As we discussed in Chapter 1, a full freezer tends to use less energy, so you are saving money while preparing for emergencies.

Water-rich fruits and vegetables found in your refrigerator crisper can keep you hydrated without reaching for drinks. Consider vegetables such as celery, cucumber, tomatoes, iceberg lettuce, radishes, and even red or green peppers. You can also eat water-rich fruit such as watermelons, cantaloupe, grapes, apples, oranges, grapefruit, and other citrus fruits that have a high water content. While you can't drink them, at least they give you some form of hydration.

Tour pantry. Don't forget that canned fruits and vegetables come packed with liquid. Save the liquid for drinking.

Toilet tank. The water found in the toilet tank is usually clean, not for drinking, but for washing. However, this water is not safe to use if you've been using cleaning tablets in the toilet tank.

Swimming pool. Most suburban neighborhoods or apartment complexes, especially in warm climates, have access to at least one swimming pool. In an emergency, you can use pool water for washing. Do not drink pool water, as it contains a large amount of bleach, water softeners, stabilizers, and possibly, salts. Without electricity running the filter, the pool water will become stagnant and eventually grow mold and mosquitoes. Many other residents will also have the same idea of using the pool water for themselves, so it is best not to rely on the pool as a water source except in extreme emergencies.

The best way to make pool water drinkable is by distilling it.

Fountains and other water features. Many subdivisions and apartment complexes have fountains, brooks, or streams to beautify the neighborhood. Unfortunately, these water features are either treated with chlorine or contain runoff from the streets. Like the swimming pool, these are not good sources of drinkable water.

Rainwater. If you live in an area that gets a lot of rain, leave containers out that can be filled with rainwater. As we discussed on page 45, rain barrels can be used for collecting rain water, but if you do not have them, use any and all available clean containers you might have on hand.

Natural bodies of water. While you still have the opportunity to explore your area during "normal" times, learn the locations of natural water sources near you, such as ponds, lakes, rivers, and streams. If a large-scale disaster happens and tap water were to stop flowing, such knowledge will be valuable for survival. Also, be aware that many city waterways are usually polluted with toxic metals, gasoline, herbicides, pesticides, and other dangerous chemicals.

When scoping out a possible water sources, remember:

- Running water is preferable to stagnant water.
- Collect water upstream instead of downstream. As water flows downstream, it is more likely to pick up sediment and pollution and is therefore likely more contaminated.
- Look at the plants surrounding the body of water: Are they healthy or dead? If all the plants around the pond are dead, the water is not safe to drink.
- Check for any dead animals. The presence of dead animals may signify the water is poisoned; alternately, if the carcass is in the water, it may have poisoned the water.

Do not drink the water until you have purified it. Getting a waterborne illness from pathogens in water will make your situation worse. Vomiting and diarrhea resulting from drinking contaminated water can cause dehydration or worse.

If you had to walk for a distance to find water, you would need portable containers and a way to transport water. Water is very heavy, so you can only carry a limited amount. Here are some ideas for inexpensive ways to transport water:

- 5-gallon buckets
- collapsible water containers
- soda and juice bottles

You may also need a wheelbarrow or cart to be able to transport the water you collected.

FILTERING WATER

Filtering water means removing any visible particles such as leaves, bugs, and dirt from the water. It does not remove any pathogens in the water, but it is the first step in making the water safe to drink.

If you are using water that has a lot of soil content, allow the sediment to settle in the bottom then pour the water into another container.

Some common materials you can use to filter water include:

- bandanna
- coffee filters
- layers of paper towels
- T-shirt

When using cloth, the tighter the weave, the better it is for filtering.

HOMEMADE WATER FILTER

You will need:

2-liter soda bottle	½ cup sand
2 to 3 cotton balls	½ cup gravel
½ cup activated carbon	

Directions:

Note: Rinse the carbon, sand, and gravel prior to the following steps.

1. Cut the bottom of the soda bottle.

2. Place the cotton balls in the lip of the bottle.

3. Place cap on loosely.

4. Pour the carbon into the inverted bottle.

5. Next, pour the sand.

6. Pour the gravel last.

7. Have another container, such as a glass, below the inverted soda bottle.

8. Pour the water down the homemade filter. It will come out much cleaner than what you started with.

DISINFECTING WATER

After filtering the solids out of your water, you then need to disinfect it to avoid catching waterborne diseases such as cholera, dysentery, hepatitis A, E. coli infection, parasitic infections, and many others. For this reason, do not use unpurified water for drinking, cooking, or brushing teeth.

HOW TO BOIL WATER IN A PLASTIC WATER BOTTLE

Ideally, a metal container is best for boiling water; however, in an emergency, you can disinfect water in a plastic water bottle. Build your fire under a tree or branch where you can suspend the water bottle. Tie a string around the neck of the bottle and suspend it from the tree or branch, about 6 inches above the fire. Fill the bottle about three-quarters full of water. The fire should start warming up the water. Gradually adjust the height of the string until the bottle is 2 inches above the fire, but not touching it. The water will start to simmer and the plastic may begin to blister. Once the water has boiled for 1 minute, move the bottle away from the fire and allow it to cool before drinking.

Boiling

As long as you have a container and fire, the simplest way to disinfect water is to boil it. Make sure the water reaches boiling point, then let it boil for at least 1 minute. I like to let it boil a bit longer, but if you are in a survival situation and need to conserve resources, a minute is all you need. It is important to note that although boiling kills germs, it does not remove salts, heavy metals, or chemical toxins. However, it is better than not doing anything at all. Boiling will leave a "flat" taste in the water as it removes the oxygen. To improve the taste, pour the water back and forth between two containers to aerate it. If you have the resources, you can also add tea, coffee, herbs, or powdered drinks to the water to improve taste.

Chlorine

Plain, unscented chlorine household bleach (5.25 percent to 5 percent concentration of sodium hypochlorite) can also be used to purify water. The rule is 2 drops of bleach to a quart of water. Or, if you have more water, use 8 drops of bleach or ⅛ teaspoon per gallon of water. Mix well then allow the water to stand for 30 minutes.

If the water is very cloudy, you may double the amounts listed above and let it stand for 30 minutes.

A couple of things to remember:

- Some brands of bleach that are concentrated (these generally show "ultra" on the label) are not appropriate for disinfecting water.

- Plain household bleach generally expires within a year and its effectiveness will diminish. Make sure you routinely rotate your supplies.

HOW TO MEASURE DROPS WITHOUT A MEDICINE DROPPER

If you have a 1-inch-long paper towel, piece of toilet paper, or cloth and a small cap of bleach, you can make a dropper. Drop some bleach on the cap. Allow the piece of paper or cloth to hang off the side of the cap and it tilt slightly so the paper is touching the bleach. The paper will act like a wick and the bleach will slowly drip off the paper in small drops.

Iodine Tincture

Iodine tincture, which is usually kept in first aid kits or medicine cabinets for treating cuts, can be used to disinfect water. Add 5 drops of iodine tincture (2 percent US) to 1 quart of water or roughly 1 liter of water (1.06 quarts=1 liter of water).

Purification Tablets

Iodine tablets: Iodine tablets are inexpensive and easily obtainable at any sporting goods store. Each tablet is usually good for a quart of water, but read the instructions before using it just to make sure you do so correctly. Iodine tablets must be stored in a dark place, as sunlight will affect the tablets.

Do not use this method of purification if:

- You are allergic to iodine or shellfish.
- You have thyroid problems or take lithium.
- You are pregnant.

Chlorine tablets: Chlorine tablets for purifying water are available at drug stores or sporting goods stores. Follow the instructions stated on the package. If you are unable to find instructions, one chlorine tablet will purify a quart of water.

Pool Shock

At first it may seem a little expensive or complicated, but using calcium hypochlorite granules, also known as pool shock, may actually be cost-effective. Why? Plain household bleach expires in a year, but pool shock has shelf life of 2-plus years if stored in proper conditions (under 95°F in a well-ventilated, non-humid area). Also, 1 pound of calcium hypochlorite granules that costs $9 to $16 will purify up to 10,000 gallons of water.

POOL SHOCK TREATMENT

Using pool shock to purify water is a multistep process. DO NOT take any shortcuts.

You will need:

78 percent granular calcium hypochlorite

measuring teaspoon

container for bleach solution

water to be purified

container for purified water

Directions:

1. Make the chlorine solution. Measure 1 teaspoon of calcium hypochlorite granules and add it to 2 gallons of

water. Mix well. This will create a bleach-like solution. Label this "Chlorine Solution: DO NOT DRINK." Mix this solution outdoors or in a well-ventilated area as it will smell heavily of chlorine. You should also write down instructions on how to use the solution to purify water.

2. To purify a batch of water, add 2½ teaspoons of chlorine solution to 1 gallon of water. Be careful not to splash yourself (especially your eyes) or clothing with this solution.

3. Let stand for 30 minutes.

4. To remove the chlorinated taste, pour the water back and forth between two containers of water.

Solar Disinfection

Another way to disinfect water is using the sun's ultraviolet rays, or solar disinfection (SODIS). Widely used in many developing countries, SODIS significantly reduces the risk of diarrhea and other waterborne diseases. It is an easy and low-tech method of disinfection.

SODIS SYSTEM

You will need:

2-liter clear plastic soda bottles

filtered water (page 49)

Directions:

1. Fill the bottles three-quarters of the way with the filtered water, place the cap on, and shake to add oxygen to the water. Take off the cap then fill to the brim before recapping.

2. Lay the bottles down in a sunny area, such as a roof. If the roof is not accessible, you may also lay the bottles down on aluminum foil.

3. The bottles should sit for a minimum of 6 hours in bright sunlight. If it is cloudy, the bottles should be exposed for 2 full days.

The ultraviolet light kills protozoa, bacteria, and viruses. However, it does not remove chemicals.

Commercial Water Purification Systems

A water purification system is an essential piece of gear for a prepper. If you are in the market for a water purifier, research the system thoroughly before you buy.

- Check the specifications of the system, such as the pore size: You should see a pore size of approximately 0.01 micron or smaller for a microfiltration system.

- Review the list of contaminants and pay attention to percentages of substances removed. The system should be able to remove protozoa (such as cryptosporidium, giardia), bacteria (examples are E. coli, salmonella, shigella), viruses (norovirus, hepatitis A), and chemicals.

- Find out about the unit's flow rates: In an emergency you will likely be purifying unclean water, which may potentially slow it down considerably.

- Purchase from a reputable source.

- Find out about return policies.

Some excellent brands include Berkey, Katadyn, and Aquamira. Water purifiers can be expensive, but there is a way to save some dollars by assembling your own.

DIY Water Purifiers

MAKE-YOUR-OWN GRAVITY-FED WATER PURIFIER

Berkey is an excellent commercial water filter, but it does come with a price. But there is a way to make your own gravity-fed water purifier using Berkey ceramic elements, which can be bought separately at a much lower cost.

You will need:

2 clean, food-grade (5-gallon) buckets with lids (can be obtained for free— see page 72)

2-pack (9-inch) Berkey ceramic filters

faucet

drill

tape measure

We will call one Bucket A and the other Bucket B; Bucket A will be sitting on top of Bucket B when this is finished.

Directions:

1. Drill a ¾-inch hole for the faucet about ½ inch from the bottom of Bucket B. Mount the faucet using the rubber rings and nut that came with it.

2. Place Bucket A upside down. On the bottom of Bucket A, drill two ½-inch holes near the center about 5 inches away from each other. This is where you will be attaching the ceramic filters.

3. On the lid of Bucket B, mark the corresponding spots where the holes were drilled in Bucket A.

4. Drill two holes on the lid of Bucket B in the places you marked in Step 3.

5. Now you can mount the ceramic filters. On each of the filters, place the rubber gaskets that came with them on to the screw.

6. Mount one filter onto a hole on Bucket A, then place on the corresponding hole of Bucket B. Use one of the mounting nuts that came with the filters to screw on the filter to the lid of Bucket B. Repeat with the other filter.

7. When the filters are screwed on properly, you are ready to use your gravity filter. Set the buckets on top of each other on a stable surface where you can access the faucet properly.

8. Fill the top bucket (Bucket A) with water. The water will slowly drip down from Bucket A to Bucket B. The water in Bucket B is purified.

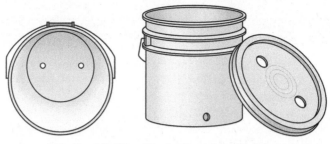

Bucket A (left) and Bucket B with lid (right)

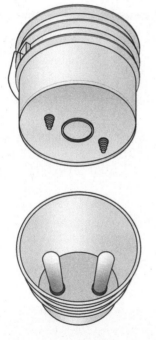

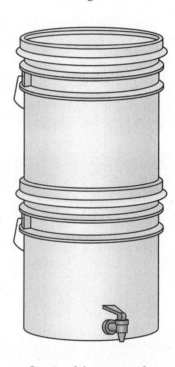

Bucket A with ceramic filters from bottom view (above) and top view (below)

Gravity-fed water purifier

WATER FILTER TEST

A good way to test if your water filter is working properly is by adding around 5 to 8 drops of food coloring to the water in Bucket A. The water in Bucket B should be completely clear if your filter is working properly.

With multiple uses, the water filter may occasionally need to be cleaned. To clean, unscrew the filters and scrub them lightly with a sponge. Rinse with cool water.

AT-HOME WATER DISTILLATION

Distillation is another effective way to remove impurities in water: It removes viruses, bacteria, protozoa, metals, and chemicals. It's a four-step process: 1. Boiling and evaporating the water, 2. Collecting the water vapor, 3. Cooling the vapor so it turns back to liquid, and 4. Collecting the water.

You will need:

water that has been filtered to remove any solids or sediment

large pot with a lid that curves out

small cup

rope or string to tie the cup to the handle of the pot

heat source such as a stove or fire pit

Directions:

1. Add filtered water to the pot until it is half full.

2. Place the lid upside-down and tie the cup to the handle of the lid.

3. Set the upside-down lid onto the pot, but make sure the cup does not touch the water you are going to boil.

4. Place the pot on your heat source and let it boil slowly.

5. Allow the water to boil for 20 minutes.

6. Turn off the heat and leave the pot alone until it cools.

7. When completely cool, you can open the lid. You will find the distilled water has collected in the cup.

CONSERVING WATER IN AN EMERGENCY

According to the U.S. Environmental Protection Agency, the average family of four uses 400 gallons of water per day. Using the toilet entails the heaviest consumption, followed by bathing, doing laundry, washing dishes, and finally, drinking and cooking.

It's a good idea to conserve water every day, but it is crucial to save water during an emergency. Repair water leaks as soon as possible. If water is scarce, you will need to use every opportunity to minimize your usage. Here are a few tips to save water every day.

Toilet and Bathroom

- Place a brick or soda bottle in the corner of the toilet tank to displace some of the water needed to flush.

- Do not run the faucet while brushing your teeth.

- While waiting for the shower to warm up, collect the cold water in a 5-gallon bucket and use it for watering plants or cleaning.

- Take short showers instead of baths.

- During emergencies: Take sponge baths instead of showers.

- Flush the toilet only for solid waste; for liquid waste, use it throughout the day before flushing.

Laundry

- Wait until you have a full load of laundry before running the washer.

Kitchen

- Prior to washing dishes by hand or using a dishwasher, scrape food off plates over the trash instead of rinsing them with tap water.

- If washing dishes by hand, plug the drain and fill the sink with soapy water instead of running the tap.

- If using a dishwasher, run the dishwasher only when it's full. You do not need to pre-rinse dishes before loading the dishwasher.

- In an emergency, collect graywater that was used for washing and use for flushing the toilet or watering plants. *Use graywater as soon as possible: Do not store it for longer than 24 hours as bacteria or mold will multiply.*

- If the tap is not running, use paper plates, cups, and disposable utensils instead of dishes.

Outdoors

- Wash your car using a bucket of water and a sponge instead of hosing it down.

- Sweep your driveway instead of using a hose to clean.

- *During emergencies when water is scarce, avoid watering the lawn.*

Conserving water every day lowers your water needs overall. Learning to use less water benefits you even if an emergency never happens. Your budget will improve as your water bill will be lower.

Chapter 3

FOOD

How much food should you store? The amount depends on the number of people in your household, how much space you have, the number of days you'd ideally like to have covered in case of emergency, and of course, your budget. Again, the question of what types of emergencies you are most concerned about will come up.

EMERGENCY FOOD

If you are just getting started, stock your food storage with a week's worth of food, then build up to 2 weeks.

A loss of electricity usually accompanies short-term emergencies such as a snowstorm, hurricane, or earthquake. Along with that comes the stress of dealing with the emergency. You'll want food that is easy to prepare and requires little or no cooking with ingredients that are readily available.

Some examples include:

- canned fruits and vegetables
- canned meats such as roast beef, Vienna sausages, corned beef hash, or Spam
- canned soups and stews
- canned tuna
- cereal
- crackers
- granola, protein, or meal replacement bars
- oatmeal
- pancake mix
- pasta
- peanut butter
- powdered milk
- ramen noodles
- rice
- spaghetti sauce
- Tang, Gatorade, or Kool-Aid drink mixes

GETTING STARTED ON YOUR FOOD-STORAGE PLAN

How long do you think you can last on the food you have, if the disaster were to happen right now? Resolve to increase the number of days you can survive without having to run to the store.

1. Take inventory of what you have now.

2. Before you start buying items for food storage, take a look at your pantry and make a note of what you already have. Most people keep a few canned soups, a few packages of pasta, pasta sauce, and perhaps, a few cans of tuna.

3. Check what you have in the refrigerator or freezer as well.

4. Track your usage.

5. Carry a notebook around with you for a week. Write down everything you used during a week's time.

6. Separate your list by category: Food, drinks, hygiene, cleaning, etc. If it is something that you use, write it down.

7. By the end of the week you will have an idea of what your household needs.

8. If you have babies, you will also need to stock up on formula and baby food.

9. Don't forget to include food for your pets.

10. Designate a space for your emergency food storage. Consider spreading out your emergency stores throughout the house. If something happens in one area, such as pest infestation, fire, or flooding, you have a better chance of salvaging some of your supplies instead of losing them all in one place.

11. Buy only food that your family will eat. A lot of people make the mistake of buying food for emergencies because they find a great sale. An emergency is not the time to be testing out strange foods. You will want food that your family will eat whether an emergency happens or not.

12. Include a few comfort foods in your supply, such as chocolate, cookies, or cheese.

13. Don't forget coffee or tea.

14. Always check expiration dates and choose the items with the furthest expiration date.

15. Include spices such as salt, pepper, sugar, Tabasco sauce, etc., as well as fats and oils (olive, vegetable, or coconut oil).

Food Storage at $10 a Week

To avoid overwhelming your budget, you can start with as little as $10 a week. Here are a few sample items that you can pick up during your weekly grocery shopping trip:

	Product	Quantity	Price
Week 1	Pinto beans	5 pounds	$2.50
	Rice	5 pounds	$2.50
	Sugar	5 pounds	$2.00
	Salt	3 canisters	$3.00
Week 2	Tuna	5 cans	$5
	Ramen noodles	12-pack	$2
	Roast beef	1 can	$3
Week 3	Corn	5 cans	$5
	Green beans	5 cans	$5
	Peaches	4 cans	$5
Week 4	Lipton noodles	5 packets	$5
	Pasta	5 packs	$5
	Spaghetti sauce	2 bottles	$5

Prices may vary by area.

CANNED FOODS AND THE RISK OF BOTULISM BACTERIA

Although canned foods last a long time, possibly well past their expiration dates, there is a point when the food goes bad and is no longer fit for consumption. I had a friend who still had cans from the '90s that actually exploded in her pantry. Canned foods that are so old they risk blowing up can be dangerous if contaminated with botulism bacteria (or *Clostridium botulinum*). Some facts about *Clostridium botulinum* contamination:

- Symptoms generally appear between 18 to 36 hours of eating a contaminated food, or possibly as early as 6 hours and up to 10 days of eating a contaminated food.

- Symptoms include difficulty breathing, double vision, difficulty swallowing, stomach cramps, nausea, vomiting, and weakness leading to paralysis.

- Infants can catch it from eating honey or corn syrup, as their digestive tracts are not fully developed to handle these foods.

- Treatment with a botulism antitoxin should be administered as soon as possible to avoid complications.

- Botulism bacteria can grow in canned foods that are damaged, warped, or very old.

- The bacteria thrives in low-salt, low-acid, high-humidity environments when food is stored without refrigeration.

- In addition to ingestion of contaminated food, it can enter the body through open wounds.

- If you suspect botulism, immediately call 911 or go to the emergency room.

To prevent any risk of contamination, throw away any old, bulging, or dented canned foods. If the canned or preserved food looks or smells "off," get rid of it. Never give babies under one year old honey or corn syrup, even to taste.

Increasing Your Storage for Long-Term Emergencies

Once you have built up your stored food to about a month's worth, consider adding bulk foods so you can stretch your food storage to cover a few months.

You can repackage the following foods to make them last for a few years:

- beans
- coffee (green coffee beans last the longest, but regular coffee can be packed as well)
- cornmeal
- hard candy
- oatmeal
- pancake mix
- pasta
- popcorn
- rice
- sugar

A note about storing flour: If you store flour with the intention of making bread, then you will need to store yeast, baking powder, etc. Stored white flour will last about 2 to 3 years in storage before it starts to develop an off taste or smell.

Where to Buy in Bulk

Besides the grocery store, the following are good sources of bulk food storage items.

WAREHOUSE STORES

Sam's Club and Costco are good sources for food storage. If you partner up with a friend or relative, you can split the cost of bulk items and split the contents as well.

DISCOUNT STORES AND PHARMACIES

Discount pharmacies such as CVS and Walgreens have a couple of food aisles where they carry canned foods, candy and chocolate, powdered drinks, and juices. Check the weekly flyer or online discounts and combine with coupons for the best deals. Walmart and Target also carry food, and if you check their weekly specials you can take advantage of sale items.

SPORTING GOODS STORES

Stores such as Academy Sports + Outdoors and REI have camping and backpacking sections that carry easy-to-prepare and portable foods. If you buy at full price, they can be expensive, but wait for the once- or twice-a-year sale to net some good discounts on food items.

ETHNIC GROCERY STORES

If you live in a big city you likely have a good selection of ethnic grocery stores to choose from. You may have seen Italian, Asian, or Middle Eastern stores on your way to work but never thought to check them out. These stores offer excellent prices on everyday food items such as pasta, rice and other grains, fresh food and meats, and canned foods. Some of the canned foods are likely made by the same brands you recognize but may be packaged differently. Don't be intimidated if the signs or labels show another language—the English translation is likely right below it; if not, just ask for help. I have frequented many of these stores and have always had a pleasant experience.

LDS CANNERY

In many major cities, the Church of the Latter Day Saints (LDS) runs food stores that sell bulk food items and materials you can store for the long term. These stores are nonprofit and offer excellent prices on items such as flour, sugar, salt, yeast, drink mixes, etc. They even teach people how to pack foods for long-term storage. You do not have to belong to the church to shop and learn; however, it is best to call ahead. Some locations may have different requirements for appointments or hours. I know there is one store in our city; however, the day I was planning to visit, I called the location and found they were closed for remodeling and were not going to reopen for several months. I was glad I called first, as it saved me an hour-long drive. For a list of stores, visit Provident Living at ProvidentLiving.org.

HEALTH FOOD STORES

Many health food stores have bulk bins for nuts, whole grains, dried fruit, etc. They also carry nutritional shakes, protein powders, and meal replacement bars that can be used for emergencies. At full price, these items can cost a lot, so watch for sales. Get to know the salespeople, as they may also give you advance notice for discount days.

Packaging Bulk Foods

To package bulk foods for long-term storage, you'll need to become familiar with a few terms.

FOOD-GRADE CONTAINERS

Anytime you store food, you must use food-grade containers. The Food and Drug Administration requires that materials that come in contact with food must not contain dyes or recycled plastic deemed harmful to humans. In addition, the material must be suitable to the food contained (i.e., acidic foods, fats, and oils will not cause the plastic to react).

If the container has been used for storage of nonfood items such as paint, plastic, soap, etc., then it is not food-grade. Therefore, you may reuse jars that previously contained rice, cereal, pancake mix, soda, or juice, but not containers that housed cat litter, detergent, etc.

Five-gallon food buckets are indispensable for food storage because they are sturdy and portable. Pests cannot chew through 5-gallon buckets.

The good news is you can get 5-gallon buckets for free: Restaurants and bakeries use a lot of items, such as condiments, pickles, icing, etc., that are packaged in these buckets. Many throw them away after using up the contents. If you know someone who works in a bakery, restaurant, or supermarket, ask them whether you can obtain some of their 5-gallon buckets. Some places may have restrictions about giving them out, but it never hurts to ask.

Once you have your buckets, wash them thoroughly with soap and water and add a few drops of bleach to sanitize. Rinse well and allow to dry. If the bucket contained pickles, it may be hard to remove the odor. You can try washing the bucket thoroughly and air dry. If that does not work, add baking soda to remove the odor. If all else fails, use the pickle-smelling buckets for storing nonfood items. Remember, do not use any container that has been used to store nonfood items.

MYLAR BAGS

You may have heard of Mylar balloons and space blankets. Mylar is actually a brand name for a type of plastic made of stretched polyester film, or "BoPET," which stands for biaxially oriented polyethylene terephthalate. It is ideal for long-term food storage because the material is chemically stable; a moisture, gas, light, and odor barrier; and strong and durable. Some vendors call their food storage bags "dry pack bags" or "metallized storage bags"—this just means the material was not manufactured by Mylar but is made of the same material.

OXYGEN ABSORBERS

Oxygen absorbers are tiny packets that contain a mixture of iron filings, salt, and clay. The clay provides moisture and works with the salt to activate the iron filings. The process starts as soon as the oxygen absorber packet is exposed to oxygen. What happens is the iron filings begin to oxidize, forming rust, which then releases nitrogen. Nitrogen helps the food keep fresher longer. The lack of oxygen in the stored food will keep weevils and other insects from living in there.

Most oxygen absorber packs come with a little pink pill that turns blue if the oxygen absorber is no longer effective. A few other notes about oxygen absorbers:

- Sugar and salt do not need oxygen absorbers as they will turn rock hard.

- Once you open a package of oxygen absorbers, you must keep the unused packs in an airtight jar, not a plastic bag, to avoid exposure to air. Otherwise they will all get activated and be useless by the time you need them.

- To be effective, you need to use the right number of oxygen absorbers for the food you are packaging. The instructions below include the type of oxygen absorber to use.

- Oxygen absorbers cannot be reused.

Now you are ready to repackage foods. Gather up your supplies.

FOOD REPACKAGING METHOD

You will need:

cardboard to place over the table (under the iron)

measuring cup

food items such as rice, pasta, pinto beans, etc.

1-gallon Mylar bags

oxygen absorbers (300 cc)

bay leaves to ward against weevils

clothes iron OR hair-straightening iron

masking tape and permanent marker for labeling

5-gallon food-grade buckets

airtight jar for keeping extra oxygen absorbers

Directions:

1. Pour 12 cups of the food item you are storing into a Mylar bag (it should be about three-quarters full).

2. Add an oxygen absorber and 1 bay leaf as you near the top of the bag. There should be about an inch of clearance from the food to the top edge of the bag.

3. Shake the Mylar bag to allow the food to settle.

4. Squeeze out any excess air.

5. Line up the sides and top of the Mylar bag.

6. If using a clothes iron, place the cardboard over your surface, then carefully iron across the top, leaving a 1-inch space open on the left corner. The iron will not stick to the Mylar; it actually stays smooth. Do not try to make a fold across the top and iron it, it will not stick

properly. "Burp" the bag to let any remaining air out. Iron across the last 1 inch remaining space and seal it up. Make sure your iron does not overheat.

7. If you are using a hair-straightening iron, *The Prepper's Guide to Food Storage* recommends leaving the bag upright and clamping the hair-straightening iron across the top, leaving an inch space open on one corner. Squeeze the last of the air out and seal the corner.

8. Label the bag with masking tape and permanent marker. Place the Mylar bag in the food-grade 5-gallon bucket. Keep packaging food items into Mylar bags following the above steps until the bucket is full. Seal up the buckets and label them with the contents and date. Store any remaining oxygen absorbers in an airtight jar.

This method will keep your stored food fresh for 5 or more years. I have personally opened up 5-year-old bulk food stored in this manner and detected no loss of quality, taste, or appearance. Some readers have reported longer periods, such as 10 to 20 years, as long as the food was properly packed.

Why not use a 5-gallon Mylar bag instead of a 1-gallon bag?
I prefer using 1-gallon bags because they can be easily opened without having to expose the rest of the food to air. If you prefer using larger bags, you can do so. One 5-gallon Mylar bag can be used to line one 5-gallon bucket. Just remember to keep the bag and bucket sealed as you use the contents.

How about vacuum-sealed bags such as FoodSaver bags?
Vacuum-sealed bags are very convenient and can be used for

food storage if you already own one. However, the bags are not as strong as Mylar bags and may leak after 3 years or so, allowing oxygen to degrade the food. If you were to vacuum seal your bulk foods, use them up within 3 years and replace.

Can Mylar bags be reused? You may have seen certain foods packed in Mylar bags, such as breadcrumbs, some cereals, and other prepackaged foods. Potato chip bags also look similar to Mylar. Potato chip bags are too thin; they would not be good for long-term food storage. However, some of the cereal and breadcrumb bags that I have seen have similar thickness to the storage bags. They can be washed, dried thoroughly, and reused. Mylar balloons and space blankets are NOT food-grade and therefore cannot be used for food.

As you open your stored foods for use, carefully cut the opening close to the top so you can reuse the Mylar bag. Make sure you wash and thoroughly dry the bags before using.

What about juice pouches? Every parent with young children has bought boxes of these juice pouches. Once empty, cut across the top. Wash and rinse the pouch. Allow to dry thoroughly. The pouch must be completely dry before you use it. You can repackage foods such as rice, pasta, and dry beans in these pouches. Fill the juice pouch about halfway, leaving room to seal. They store about half a cup of dry foods. Include a pouch with sugar, salt, or other spices as well. They can be used for short-term storage, such as overnight camping trips, car survival kits, or dorm rooms. You will still need a pot and some water to boil in an emergency.

BARGAIN STORAGE METHOD

Use recycled food containers such as sanitized 2-liter soda or juice bottles with oxygen absorbers.

In Chapter 3, we discussed storing water in clean 2-liter bottles. You can use them for food storage as well. This method will not last as long as the Mylar bag method, but is a good substitute if you are on a tight budget. You just need to be mindful of the dates. If using recycled containers, use up your storage within 2 to 3 years, as these containers will eventually leak and allow oxygen in.

You will need:

1 (2-liter) bottle	100 cc oxygen absorber

Directions:

1. Using a funnel, fill the 2-liter bottle with the food you are repackaging, such as rice or oats. Add the oxygen absorber right before you cap the bottle.

2. Label each bottle with permanent marker to indicate the date stored.

Enemies of Food Storage

Before getting further into our discussion, we need to take a look at what can ruin your food storage.

Air. The oxygen in the air encourages growth of bacteria and insects. Removing most of the oxygen when storing food will help extend its shelf life. We will go over how to do this later in the chapter.

Heat. I am sure you have noticed that foods spoil much more quickly during the summer. That is because heat encourages spoilage. Ideally, stored food should be kept at a temperature of 40°F to 72°F. If kept at high temperatures, food will lose much of its nutritional value, taste, texture, and appearance. However, this does not mean you cannot store food if you live in a warm climate with no air conditioning. It just means you should use your stored food at a quicker rate and replace it with new stock. It is always a good idea to rotate your food continuously.

Light. Foods kept in direct sunlight will degrade much more quickly than foods stored in the dark. That's because light alters the chemical composition of the food as well as the packaging, causing both to degrade more quickly.

Moisture or humidity. Stored food should stay as dry as possible. If you live in a humid area, using an air conditioner or dehumidifier will help keep humidity at bay. Avoid storing food on the floor, next to open windows, or near cracks where humidity can get in.

Pests. Depending on where you live, you may have insects, rodents, or both. Sometimes, microscopic insect larvae may be present in dry goods, such as flour. You've likely seen weevils in old flour. You can avoid this problem by placing the bag of flour in the freezer for 4 to 5 days prior to storing to make sure nothing hatches. Always keep the area around your food storage clean. Before you even get started, you need to make sure your area is rodent-free. Rats can also be a problem, as they are attracted to food and will chew through most containers.

Time. Food goes bad after a period of time and can become unfit for eating. Foods that are high in fats and oils get rancid more quickly than dry foods do. The solution is to always rotate your food storage; use the older items first and keep replenishing.

Chemical contamination. Storing foods that are not properly packaged next to chemicals that give off odors can potentially ruin the food. Fumes may penetrate through paper, cardboard, or even flimsy plastic packaging.

Finally, there is also the risk that someone in your household may eat through your stash without your knowing about it. Kids will eat up cereals or snack foods that are kept in storage and snack on them without telling anyone. To avoid surprises like this, we just tell our kids to let us know if they finished up the last of a food item, or to add it to the grocery list that is posted on the refrigerator.

FOOD STORAGE SAFETY TIPS

- Rotate your stored food. Use the oldest items first. This is called the "first in, first out" system for your inventory.

- Use a permanent marker to write down the expiration date on the package where you can see it easily.

- Store the items with the closest expiration dates in the front of your pantry and items with the furthest expiration dates in the back.

- Set a minimum limit for each item you will have on hand. For example, you may want to always have 12 cans of canned corn.

- As you use up the items in front, replace them with new items.

- Most foods do not expire on the exact date indicated on the package; however, using them up as they approach expiration ensures that you will always have the freshest stock and helps you avoid waste.

- Store your emergency foods in a clean, dry area.

- In any room where food is stored, keep the temperature constant at 70°F to 75°F maximum. Excessive heat causes food to spoil faster, so if you live in a warm climate, do not store your emergency food in the garage.

- Keep stored food away from direct sunlight; being exposed to light also shortens the shelf life of food.

- Make sure the area is pest-free.

- Don't store food near hazardous chemicals or anything that gives off fumes. This could also ruin your stored food.

CAN YOU STILL PREP IF YOU ARE ON PUBLIC ASSISTANCE?

I have been asked by readers whether people on public assistance can prepare for emergencies. Food stamps or SNAP (Supplemental Nutrition Assistance Program) can only be used to buy food.

WHAT ABOUT FREEZE-DRIED FOOD?

Freeze drying is a process used to remove all moisture from the food to retard spoilage. This increases its shelf life by 10 to 20 years or possibly more. Freeze drying also shrinks the food and makes it considerably lighter.

Many companies sell freeze-dried food for survival and emergency preparedness, as well as for backpacking and camping. They are simple to use and relatively quick to prepare. However, these foods can be costly. Try smaller packages before buying large quantities.

Some food storage companies offer free or nearly free samples of their products, sometimes just charging for postage. If you are interested in trying before you buy, periodically search online for "free samples food storage." Check out the companies who are offering and find out what the requirements are. Read the small print. Do not buy if you have to sign up for membership or if you will get charged for any recurring orders.

The USDA website says SNAP benefits can be used to buy:

- breads and cereals
- fruits and vegetables
- meats, fish, and poultry
- dairy products
- seeds and plants that can be used to produce food

They cannot be used to buy:

- hot foods
- alcoholic beverages, including beer, wine, and liquor
- tobacco
- pet food
- soaps, paper products, or toilet paper
- vitamins and minerals
- soft drinks, candy, cookies, snack crackers, and ice cream
- bakery cakes

Therefore, going by the description of benefits, as long as you buy food within the allowed category, you can use these benefits to buy food for emergencies.

The key would be to maximize what you can buy using the following tips:

- Review each grocery store's weekly ads for the best sales.
- Use coupons and combine them with what's on sale.
- Visit different stores that are close to each other and buy the "loss leaders." These are heavily discounted items that draw shoppers to the store.
- Because you can use these benefits for seeds, start a small garden to supplement your family's diet.

HANDLING FOOD DURING A POWER OUTAGE

If you lose electricity, keep the refrigerator and freezer doors closed to help prevent food spoilage. Then, deal with various categories of foods as follows.

Meats and Other Perishables

Here are two rules of thumb regarding refreezing meat if you have a power outage:

1. If the meat still has ice crystals and the fridge temperature stayed at around 40°F, then it is safe to refreeze.

2. If the power was out less than 4 hours and the fridge or freezer door was kept closed, then the food will still be safe.

However, if you have any doubts, it may be best to throw it out. It is not worth getting sick from bad food.

You cannot always tell by taste and smell; bacteria may have grown on the food that cannot be detected by taste or smell. Besides, if you taste the food that has already spoiled, you may get sick just from tasting it. Throw out any perishable foods that have been kept at above 40°F for 2 hours.

As much as you may hate wasting food, your health is not worth risking.

Can you store freezer food out in the snow if you lose power during a snowstorm? Placing perishable food out in the snow does not guarantee it will be safe to eat. Temperatures outside rarely remain constant: Food can thaw, and the sun may warm up parts of the food, causing bacteria to grow. The food can also come in contact with animals or insects.

Instead, place the food in a cooler and pack it with snow. Or make your own ice by leaving water bottles outside to freeze and using those to keep your food cold.

EGGS

Fresh eggs can last for a few weeks in the refrigerator, but you can make them last even longer with this simple process. You will need mineral oil, which be found in the stomach remedy aisle in the grocery store or pharmacy.

Inspect each egg for any cracks or holes. Do not include these eggs in your preserving project, as they will get rotten quickly.

Rub about a quarter-size drop of mineral oil all over each egg so that it is completely covered. Store the eggs in the original container and turn them over every week to keep the oil from pooling in one spot.

If you've had eggs in the fridge for so long you are not sure they are still fresh, use this easy test to find out. Fill a deep bowl with cool water. Carefully place the egg in the water. If the egg sinks and lies on its side, it is fresh. If it stands up and bobs slightly, it is not so fresh, but still consumable. If it floats then it is rotten.

Fruits

Without refrigeration, the shelf life of fruit depends on when the fruit was picked and how ripe it was when you bought it. Many fruits last a long time without refrigeration: Apples and citrus fruits will last around 4 to 5 weeks on the counter.

Ripe pineapples and mangoes must be eaten within 24 hours.

Strawberries and other berries are short-lived without the fridge. Eat them as soon as possible, or the following day after the power outage at the latest.

Vegetables and Herbs

If you don't have power for some time, herbs and some vegetables, such as celery, broccoli, and cauliflower, will stay fresh when stored upright in some water.

Root crops, such as potatoes, sweet potatoes, onion, and garlic, will last 1 to 2 months without refrigeration. Cut onions will need to be used right away or they will get moldy.

Squash such as zucchini will last a week.

Tomatoes (technically a fruit but considered a vegetable for cooking purposes) will last 2 weeks if they are still green, or about a week at the most if they are already ripe.

MAKING YOUR OWN MEALS READY TO EAT

Meals Ready to Eat (MREs) are portable meals used by the military. What's in an MRE? MREs contain everything needed for one meal, including starches, a meat entrée, fruit or vegetable, a drink mix, crackers, seasoning packets containing salt, pepper, and Tabasco sauce, a mint, coffee, and tea. A heating unit is included as well. MREs are convenient and filling, both great advantages in an emergency. However, at $7 to $9 each, MREs can be expensive.

I like the concept of having easy-to-prepare meals for an emergency, so we will use that idea and make our own. Here are two ways to make your own MREs.

Prepackaged Assembly

You will need gallon-size zip-top bags. For the best pricing, buy these items on sale or with coupons. Purchase a variety of the following foods according to your preferences.

Meal	Product
Breakfast	instant oatmeal, dried fruits, nuts, granola bars, breakfast bars
Lunch	instant soup or ramen noodles, easy-to-open packets of tuna, cheese spread, crackers
Dinner	meat spreads, crackers, chicken or other meats such as Spam, tuna steaks in a pouch, Hormel Compleats, packets of instant mashed potatoes
Snacks	dried fruit-and-nut mixes, individually packed fruit cups
Miscellaneous	salt and pepper, eating utensils, napkins or wipes, instant coffee, tea bags, mints or other hard candy, matches or lighters, portable stove, and small pot for heating water

Assemble the meals by placing them in 1-gallon zip-top bags for each member of the family. Remove as much air as possible from each pack. If you have a food sealer, you can use that instead of the gallon-size zip-top bags. You will also need bottled water for preparing instant soups and for drinking.

These meals are suitable for consumption either at home or on the road.

"Just Add Water" Meals

Another way to make instant meals is to assemble your own meals in a jar using dehydrated foods (page 264). For example, for a pot of chicken soup, include the following ingredients in a jar or in an airtight pouch:

⅛ cup dried onion

¼ cup dried celery

¼ cup dried carrots

2 chicken bouillon cubes

dash of dried parsley

egg or ramen noodles

1 (6- to 12.5-ounce) can chicken (optional)

Directions:

1. Add an oxygen absorber to the jar. Remove the oxygen absorber and discard before cooking.

2. When ready to use, add 8 cups of water to the above mixture and simmer for 15 to 20 minutes until the vegetables and noodles are softened.

3. Add a can of chicken during the last 5 minutes of cooking. This recipe makes about five to six servings of soup.

You can make variations to this recipe such as using beef bouillon instead of chicken and using canned beef.

Now you have a meal ready to eat. Serve with crackers.

These meals should last approximately a year in your pantry. You can even use them on busy weeknights instead of going out for fast food.

SAVE MONEY ON FOOD

In this section, we will cover the biggest source of waste in most households: food waste. US households are said to throw out about 25 percent of the food they buy. I believe the number is at least that much, perhaps more. I used to throw out a lot of food myself, usually produce that got rotten before I could use it. Now I am a lot more careful and try to avoid waste as much as possible.

Most people are well-meaning and don't really set out to let good food spoil. But it still happens and is a huge waste of money. I know the routine: You cook the meal and have a lot left over. Trying to be good, you package it in plastic containers and store it in the fridge, intending to eat the leftovers. Unfortunately, the family may not want to eat the leftovers, or you have a lunch meeting the next day and the leftover food sits uneaten. The desire to eat it diminishes with each passing day and soon you have to throw it out.

In addition to saving you money, learning to avoid waste also helps you manage your resources in a disaster situation, making your supply last as long as possible. Here are some tips to avoid wasting food:

BEWARE OF THE BULGE

Discard any canned foods that are bulging or corroded; these are unsafe to eat and may cause botulism. If you hang on to old, bulging cans long enough, they may eventually leak or explode and will cause a huge, smelly mess in your pantry. Also, use your senses when you open canned food. If it looks or smells strange or even a little "off," it is best to discard it.

Packaged Foods

Avoid confusion about food date labels. A lot of consumers throw out food based on the date given on the label. However, the date does not necessarily signify that the food has gone bad as soon as the date has passed.

The "sell by" date tells the retailer how long to keep the item on the store shelf. It does not mean the item becomes spoiled right after that date; it just indicates it may have passed its peak of freshness.

The terms "best if used by" and "best before" refer to the product's best flavor or quality. Passing the date does not mean the item is no longer edible.

The "use by" date is determined by the manufacturer to signify when the product has passed its peak in freshness or quality.

Rotate your canned and packaged foods with the first in, first out system, using the oldest items first.

Fresh Foods

Don't wash fruits and vegetables until you are ready to use them. The moisture causes them to rot faster.

I have found that vegetables such as celery, spinach, zucchini, and even herbs such as cilantro, green onions, etc., last longer when wrapped in paper towels. The paper towel absorbs moisture. This method can keep the vegetables from wilting or getting mushy for about 3 to 4 days.

Freeze uneaten fruits and vegetables before they go bad. Frozen watermelon and cantaloupe can be made into shakes or slushies. Frozen bananas can be eaten frozen, used as a base for shakes, or mashed up to make muffins. Freeze grapes for a refreshing treat. Fresh corn can be frozen for later use. Tomatoes can also be frozen to make into fresh salsa later. Chop up onion, peppers, zucchini, and other types of squash to freeze and use later.

Dairy

Milk will safely last a week past the "sell by" date. You can tell milk has gone bad if it has solid bits floating in it or smells funky. Yogurt can last up to a month after the date stamped. To make dairy products such as yogurt, sour cream, and ricotta cheese stay fresher longer, store them upside down in the refrigerator.

HOW TO FREEZE MILK

Milk can be frozen for later use. Buy multiple containers whenever milk goes on sale. Open each container and empty out about an inch or two to allow for expansion. Freeze the milk. To use, leave the milk container in the refrigerator overnight or place it in a pan of water to thaw in the sink for 4 hours. I have tried it both ways and did not notice much of a difference in the taste of the milk. You can store milk for 1 to 2 months in the freezer without any noticeable difference. I have not stored it for longer periods and therefore cannot attest to the results.

Cooking

Much of wasted food can be avoided by planning menus and quantities properly, based on your family's eating preferences.

- If you know your family never eats leftovers and you are always having to throw out food, cook smaller portions.

- Serve younger children smaller servings. A lot of waste comes from kids being unable to finish what is served. If they want seconds, they will ask for more.

- Resolve to eat leftovers the very next day. Or, have a buffet night where family members get to choose which leftover dish to eat up.

- Make something else out of the food you cook. Make croutons from stale bread; make soup stock out of chicken or beef bones.

- Freeze small portions of leftover food such as vegetables, small bits of chicken, or beef. When you have a good amount, combine these ingredients with broth and herbs and spices such as a bay leaf, parsley, salt, and pepper, and you have soup.

- Leftover wine can be frozen in ice cube trays for use in pasta sauce and other dishes requiring wine.

- If you have chicken, turkey, or beef bones, make soup stock by adding onion, garlic, a bay leaf, and your favorite spices and simmer for 1 hour. Use a colander and strain out the bones. Refrigerate or freeze the soup stock for later use.

- Get every last bit from containers: Store the bottles upside down. For peanut butter, mayonnaise, jelly, and other jars, use a rubber spatula to scrape the sides for a final use.

JUST ADD WATER!

This tip can help you stretch a lot of ingredients and use up every last drop. I was running low on ketchup and I remembered a trick my grandparents used to do. Whenever they were about to run out of something, they'd add a bit of water and shake up the bottle. I had forgotten all about it until recently. I added just ⅛ cup of water to the ketchup bottle and no one noticed. I did the same thing to my dishwashing liquid. Don't add too much or it will get overly diluted.

Groceries

The grocery store is a pitfall for many shoppers. Avoid going over budget on your weekly shopping expedition with the following tips.

Pay cash for groceries and don't bring your credit or debit card. This is a tough one but it works for me. I frequently get tempted to go over budget just seeing delicious foods, especially at stores with good samples. To counteract the temptation, I leave my cards at home and bring the budgeted amount of cash. The fear of being embarrassed at not having enough money when I pay at the cashier stops me from going over budget. As you shop, you must add up everything in your cart, including taxable items.

Create a menu for each day of the week. Include breakfast, lunch, dinner, and snacks. Check your pantry for ingredients you may already have, then list all the ingredients that you need. Stick to your list when you shop!

Always check the price per unit. Most supermarkets post the unit price right below the price of the item. If not, you will need to calculate it by taking the price and dividing it by the number of ounces (or pounds or whatever measurement is used). Bulk items do not always have the lowest price per unit. Not too long ago, I was shopping for butter. I thought the four quarter sticks would have a lower price per unit than the two quarter sticks. When I compared the costs per unit, the two-stick package was actually cheaper than the four-stick package.

Check the bulk bins. Many grocery stores have bulk bins for nuts, flour, sugar, and spices. Some shoppers avoid them for fear of germs from people measuring out the items by hand. That is certainly a valid concern, but upon inspection, I noticed that many of the bulk dispensers are sealed and can be measured out by turning a lever instead of a manual scoop. Pricing for bulk items are much lower than prices for the prepackaged versions.

Watch those weekly flyers. The flyers show the loss leaders, items that are priced low to get you in the door in the hopes that you will buy much more than the sale items. Of course it works, because most people will go ahead and buy the nonsale items. Take advantage of loss leaders by buying multiples. If you use coupons, combine them with the sale items for even bigger savings.

Eat a snack before going grocery shopping. If you shop while you are hungry, you will end up overspending on groceries, especially prepared convenience foods that catch your eye.

Chapter 4

SHELTER AND COMFORT

When sheltering during an emergency, the most likely place you will find yourself during a disaster is your home. Most people would prefer to be at home with their family if an emergency were to happen. Your home is your sanctuary and therefore should remain as comfortable as possible as you huddle together in a disaster.

LIGHTING

In an emergency, power will likely be interrupted. If you're not prepared, you can get caught in the difficult situation of navigating the darkness, especially when night comes. Light provides comfort and safety and you will want to make sure you have several backup sources.

Stock up on flashlights (with batteries), oil lamps, camp lanterns, candles, and matches. You should also have tap lights in dark areas of your home, such as the attic, garage, and closets so you can easily tap them on to avoid accidental slips or bumps.

Another great option for emergency lighting is the camp headlamp. The headlamp allows you to have light with you at all times while keeping your hands free to do chores, carry kids, or anything else that needs doing. They are inexpensive and last for a long time. You should have one for each member of your family. Keep all your backup lighting gear in an easy-to-find area that you can easily reach in the dark.

Waterproof matches are available for purchase, but you can make regular matches waterproof by doing it yourself.

HOMEMADE WATERPROOF MATCHES

You will need:

sheets of old newspaper or plastic sheets

box of wooden matches

nail polish (any color)

Directions:

1. Cover your work area with newspaper or plastic sheets.

2. Take a matchstick and paint the head of the match about halfway down with nail polish.

3. Note: Another method is to dip the match directly into the nail polish about halfway, but this method tends to cause more drips. I prefer painting it to remove excess polish.

4. Lay it flat with the painted heads suspended on the edge of the table to dry. Place a piece of paper on the floor under the table to catch drips. Repeat steps 1 to 3 for each of the matchsticks.

5. Once dry, you can repackage them in the matchbox.

That's it! I have tested homemade waterproof matches and found them to work well, even after they have gotten soaked. The paper matches do not work well, so use only wooden matches if you are going to try this.

Emergency Lamps from Common Household Items

If you find yourself in a power outage and are away from your supplies, you can improvise and make your light source from common household items. As with any items involving fire, do not leave these lamps or any other homemade lamp unattended; keep out of reach of children and pets.

SODA CAN AND OIL LAMP

You will need:

aluminum soda can

torch oil or olive oil

strip of cotton T-shirt material cut in same length of the can and rolled

matches or lighter

Directions:

1. Cut the aluminum can in half.

2. Fill the lower half of the can with torch oil or olive oil.

3. Take your rolled wick and dip it in the oil. Securely fit the top part of the can over the bottom half while slipping the wick out of the soda can's opening.

4. Light the wick.

VEGETABLE OIL AND SALT LAMP

You will need:

baby food jar or votive candle jar

table salt

½ cup vegetable oil

wooden toothpick

cotton (must be 100 percent cotton, not a blend)

nail polish remover

matches or lighter

Directions:

1. Fill the jar with table salt.

2. Use a teaspoon to add most of the vegetable oil and mix well with the salt. Let it settle down.

3. When the vegetable oil settles, add the remainder of the ½ cup.

4. Wrap a wooden toothpick with the cotton from end to end. Do not skimp on cotton, but don't make it too thick either.

5. Stick the cotton-wrapped toothpick in the vegetable oil/salt mixture. If it is too tall for the jar, simply snip the end with a pair of scissors or nail clippers until the tip is level with the mouth of the jar.

6. Drop a tiny amount of nail polish remover on the tip of the cotton-wrapped toothpick. Take care not to spill it into the vegetable oil.

7. Light the tip.

This homemade lamp will burn for about 2 hours.

Source: *Book 2: Olive Oil Lamps &c.* by Ron Brown

Variation to the vegetable oil and salt lamp: If you have a can of Crisco shortening in your pantry, you can use it to make a light source. Scoop some Crisco into your candle jar. Use a toothpick as the wick. Light the wick. While the Crisco stays solid, your wick will stay upright. Lard or bacon grease can also substitute for Crisco.

COTTON BALL AND OIL LAMP

You will need:

cotton ball

vegetable oil

baby food jar, votive candle jar, or tuna can

aluminum foil

matches or a lighter

flammable solution (you can use a drop of nail polish, nail polish remover, or petroleum jelly)

Directions:

1. Soak the cotton ball with vegetable oil, then place the cotton ball in your container. Shape a little tip on one side of the cotton ball. This will be your wick.

2. Cut a piece of aluminum foil to the size of a nickel and poke a small hole in the middle with a pencil.

3. Pull the tip of the cotton ball through the hole in the aluminum foil.

4. Place a drop of flammable solution (petroleum jelly, nail polish remover, or nail polish) on the cotton ball tip.

5. Light the cotton ball wick.

This lamp should last for a couple of hours.

I realize there are cheaper fuels than vegetable oil, but it is good to know how to make lamps from easy-to-find materials in case of emergency.

Source: *Book 2: Olive Oil Lamps &c.* by Ron Brown

Low-Cost Solar Lights

Solar garden lights, commonly found at home improvement stores, are an inexpensive option for emergency lighting. A pack of eight solar garden lights typically costs $20 to $30 and lasts for a long time.

You can either keep a set just for emergencies or line your yard with everyday solar lights that charge up during the day, taking them inside in the case of a power outage. In my experience, solar lights typically last for about two years of constant use.

POWER SOURCES

Batteries

You will need to store plenty of batteries of varying sizes to fit your flashlights. An economical option is to purchase rechargeable batteries and keep them charged just in case. They may be more expensive up front than regular batteries but can save money in the long run.

Most households are likely to have batteries lying around that may or may not be any good. Investing in a battery tester will help you save money on batteries. I recently bought one for $6 and change. Afterward, do the following:

- Gather up all your old batteries from the junk drawer, car glove box, and anywhere else you may find them.

- Start testing all your old batteries and separate them into three piles: Good, low, replace.

- Save the "good" ones and get rid of the ones in the "low" or "replace" piles.

- Discard any batteries that appear to be leaking or broken.

If you don't have a battery tester, there is a free way to test whether a battery is dead:

Drop the battery from a few inches above a hard surface. The good battery makes a thumping sound and will not bounce. It may even stand on its own. If the battery bounces, it is likely to be a dead battery.

However, this is only an improvised test—using a battery tester is the best way to test batteries.

Portable Solar Chargers

In the last few years, portable solar chargers have become very affordable. When they first came out, they cost over $100, but now that the technology is more commonly available, many portable solar charger are under $50.

You can find solar-powered battery chargers, but more importantly, you should keep a backup solar charger for your cell phone and other USB devices such as tablets, Kindle, Nook, etc.

When comparing features, read reviews and pay attention to how fast the solar charger is said to charge and its weight, portability, overcharge protection system (to prevent your device from overcharging), construction (weatherproof, waterproof), number of charging ports, and types of devices it will charge.

Generators

A discussion of power sources would not be complete without mentioning a generator. Generators are highly sought during hurricane season and quickly disappear from store shelves anytime an emergency is expected. Certainly, a generator will keep a few appliances, such as the refrigerator, running in the event of a power outage. However, they also have a few challenges that you need to be aware of before you start shopping for one:

- Generators are noisy. If you run a generator during an emergency when everyone else has no power, everyone will hear the noise and you may attract unwanted attention.

- Depending on the power source, the generator may give off fumes. They must never be used in enclosed spaces as there is a risk of carbon monoxide poisoning.

- Many generators are extremely heavy. If you expect to be moving it around, you will need one with wheels, and added features usually add to the price.
- If you buy a gasoline or diesel generator, you must have a safe way to store fuel.
- Generators are usually not allowed in apartments, townhomes, or condominiums due to restrictions against storing fuel, as well as the noise and fumes mentioned above.

I am not in any way trying to convince you that generators are a bad idea—they do have a lot of benefits. However, before I did research and owned a generator, I was not aware of all the facts. If you do decide to go ahead and purchase a generator, research the following features:

Fuel source. A gasoline generator is the most common type of generator. You can also buy a diesel generator instead of one that runs on regular gas. Diesel can be stored for longer periods that regular gasoline; however, it may not be readily available in some areas.

Propane and natural gas generators are also available. They do not produce as many fumes as gasoline and diesel; however, the canisters can be dangerous if they were to spring a leak.

Solar generators are less common and offer the least risk; however, they are the most expensive type of generator.

SAFETY PROCEDURES FOR STORING FUEL

Use self-venting canisters that have a no-spill spout. Store only small amounts (less than 10 gallons) in a cool, dark place. Garages that overheat are not good places to store gasoline due to the risk of fire. Gasoline fumes can be dangerous and will permeate other items that may be stored nearby. Never smoke or operate appliances near stored gasoline.

Installation. You should hire a licensed electrician to install your generator.

Power. How much power does the generator produce? Each generator is different: Read the manual for the wattage calculation table, along with wattage calculation charts, which give the "running watts" and the "additional start-up watts" for common household appliances such as the refrigerator/freezer, computer/monitor, air conditioner, etc.

Space. Decide on a space for the generator before buying one. Remember that it needs a well-ventilated area and cannot be inside a home, shed, or garage. Even if you leave a window or garage door a crack open, the ventilation will not be sufficient against fumes.

Starting the generator. It can have an electric start, which requires a battery, a recoil start (done by turning on the engine then pulling the starter handle gently until resistance is felt), or a combination of both.

Price. Cost for generators can range from a couple hundred to over a thousand dollars, depending on the features. Carefully weigh the price you can afford versus the features and appliances it will help you run before making your choice.

WARMTH

This section will help you stay comfortable without power during temperature extremes. If you lose power during the winter, you will need to find alternate ways to warm up your space.

Line your windows. One of the causes of cold seeping into your space may be flimsy or leaky windows. Double-paned windows work best to keep heat in but what can you do when faced with a cold snap and you do not have the time or funds to reinforce your windows? Insulate them! Here are a few ways to insulate drafty windows:

- **Window films.** Home improvement stores carry window films that you can install yourself. The drawback is they are not cheap, and if you rent your home or apartment, you may not want to make this type of alteration.

- **Bubble wrap.** Bubble wrap is fairly inexpensive and can be obtained for free if you keep all the bubble wrap your packages are mailed in. All you have to do is line the inner side of your windows with bubble wrap, then use painter's tape to secure the bubble wrap against the window. It does not look any different from the outside, but it does obscure some of your view when you look out from the inside.

- **Plastic wrap.** You can also use plastic wrap instead of bubble wrap. It is thinner but adds another layer to your windows to keep the warmth inside.

- **Trash bags.** Finally, you can use trash bags to line your windows. The disadvantage is your rooms will be darkened, especially if you use black trash bags. However, as a temporary measure, it works.

Insulate your walls. Hang blankets, comforters, or large towels against your walls or use them as curtains to keep the room warm.

Set up a warm room. If you have no power, gather all your family members in one room and make it the warmest one. Set up tents and sleeping bags in the middle of the room.

Dress in layers. Dressing in several layers of clothing creates insulating air pockets that keep you warmer than one thick coat. Don't forget to protect your head, hands, and feet. Layer old socks inside your gloves and shoes. You may feel and look bulky, like the kid in *A Christmas Story*, but you'll be warm.

Layer your bed. Use flannel sheets instead of cotton. Pile on multiple blankets, comforters, or even towels and clothes over your bed.

Shop garage sales and thrift stores during the warmer months for inexpensive blankets and comforters. Wash and store in time for winter.

Drink warm liquids. Warm up from the inside by drinking hot tea, coffee, or cocoa.

Use a propane heater. A small propane heater such as Mr. Heater Buddy Indoor-Safe Portable Radiant Heater is a good backup heater in the event of a power outage during winter.

DIY HEATER

This DIY heater works because the inner flower pot gets very hot, trapping hot air in between the two pots. The heat then escapes out of the drain hole of the larger pot, thus warming the room.

Before trying this out, make sure you have a safe, stable area on which to place the makeshift heater. Keep out of the reach of children and pets that can potentially knock this over.

You will need:

4 tea lights, including metal casings

loaf pan

2 clay flower pots, a small and one larger that can nest the smaller one

aluminum foil (optional)

Directions:

1. Place the 4 lighted tea lights in the bread loaf tin.

2. Cover them with a small flower pot turned upside down.

3. Cover the drain hole of the pot with a metal casing from one of the tea lights, or use aluminum foil.

4. Take the larger pot and place it over the small flower pot, leaving the drain hole uncovered.

SAFETY TIPS FOR BACKUP HEAT SOURCES

Whether your portable heater is store-bought or homemade, always observe the following safety tips:

- Turn off the portable heater when you leave the room or go to bed.

- Always keep a perimeter of 3 feet around the heater that is free of anything that can potentially burn.

- The air around the immediate area of the heater can get very hot. Keep kids and pets from getting too close.

- Read the operating manual thoroughly before using the heater.

- Use only the recommended fuel for your type of heater.

- Make sure your space is well-ventilated.

What not to do:

- Never heat your home using your oven.

- Do not try to warm up your home using your gas stove. Enough people get tempted to try this and every year, there are news reports of families falling asleep with the gas stove on, resulting in fatal results due to carbon monoxide poisoning.

- Do not try to use a generator improperly in an enclosed space.

STAYING COOL

It can be just as miserable to lose electricity during the worst heat of summer. Having no air conditioning when temperatures reach 100°F or above can be life-threatening. Here are several ways to stay cool:

- Drink plenty of fluids.

- Eat lighter meals: Choose vegetables and fruits instead of fatty foods.

- Limit outdoor activities to the early morning or late evening hours.

- Wet a scarf or bandanna and wear it around your neck. Or, buy a cooling scarf that has water-storing crystals. They work by pre-soaking the scarves in cool water. The crystals expand as they absorb water and cool you when you wear it. When working outdoors, pace yourself and take breaks in the shade frequently.

- Wear a hat and sunscreen.

- Don't forget the pets—keep them hydrated as well.

- Keep a spritzer bottle full of water and spray yourself every now and then.

- You can keep your bed cool by using cotton sheets and spraying them with water.

EASY PROJECT: COOLING NECK SCARF

You will need:

scissors

¼ yard of pre-washed cotton cloth

water-storing crystals found at craft stores like Michael's or Hobby Lobby

needle and thread, or sewing machine

Directions:

1. Cut fabric into two 4 x 40-inch strips. Fold the fabric lengthwise with the wrong side of the fabric out. You are making long tubes.

2. Sew across the length (starting an eighth of an inch from the edge) of the fabric with tight, fine stitches (tight stitching ensures the crystals do not fall out), and leave the ends open. If you are hand sewing, you might want to re-stitch across.

3. Now you can turn the fabric right side in.

4. Iron the tube, with the seam in the center.

5. Fold the tube in half. Stitch the halfway mark to separate one side from the other.

6. Use a funnel and add ¼ teaspoon of crystals on either side of the middle stitch. Don't be tempted to add more; these crystals swell up with water and may burst your seams.

7. Measure 4½ inches from the center and stitch vertically as you did in the center. Add ¼ teaspoons of crystals.

8. Measure another 4½ inches and stitch again. Add ¼ teaspoons of crystals on both sides. You will have four pockets of crystals.

9. Now you can stitch the ends to close them up.

   To use, soak the scarves overnight in cold water. They will swell to two or three times their size. Wrap the scarf around your neck for a cooling effect. Pets love them too.

COOKING WITHOUT ELECTRICITY

During extended emergencies, you will need to be able to cook food without power.

Gas stoves. If you have gas in addition to electricity, gas utilities may continue to operate during an emergency, allowing you to use your gas stove. However, in the event that gas is also out, you will need to rely on other backup ways to cook.

Barbecues. If you have a barbecue grill, it can double as an emergency method for cooking, as long as you have charcoal briquets.

Camp stoves. There is a wide variety of camp and backpacking stoves available, such as propane stoves, butane stoves, or combinations of both. Buy them at end-of-summer sales for maximum discounts, or shop at garage sales or thrift shops for a fraction of the original price.

Solar cookers. Solar cookers, or ovens, will cook anything that a traditional oven or stove can using the power of the sun. Leave the dish inside the solar cooker to slowly cook all day, adjusting it occasionally to make sure it continues to face the sun.

DIY ROCKET STOVE

A rocket stove is an efficiently designed stove that cooks with much less fuel, emits less smoke, and burns hotter than a traditional open fire. Rocket stoves can cost $60 to over $100 depending on the brand, but you can make your own using common household materials.

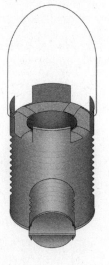

You will need:

#10 can with lid

3 (28-ounce) cans

marker

metal cutting tool

insulation, such as leftover attic insulation

heavy-duty gloves

wire hanger

heat-resistant paint (optional)

Directions:

1. Make the center hole in the #10 can. Use a lid from one of the 28-ounce cans and draw a circle on the lower section of the #10 can. Use your metal cutting tool to cut out the circle. (See Figure 1.)

2. Fit the 28-ounce can in the hole you just made. (See Figure 2.)

3. Now it is time to cut a hole in the 28-ounce can that will be going inside the #10 can. Use the piece you just cut out of the #10 can and measure a circle on the side of one of the 28-ounce cans. Cut out the hole. Cut and insert the second 28-ounce can. (See Figure 3.)

4. Cut off the rim of the last 28-ounce can. Make 1½-inch tabs around the top of the can.

5. Squeeze the tabbed end into the box cans. (See Figure 4.)

6. Fold some of the tabs up to secure it. (See Figure 5.)

7. Cut the lid. Using the last 28-ounce can, trace a circle in the middle of the #10 can lid. Then cut it out. You will be using the outer circle with the hole in it. (See Figure 6.)

8. Insulate. Cut tabs around the large can. Place insulating material around the small 28-ounce can inside the #10 can. Fit as much insulation as you can. (See Figures 7 and 8.)

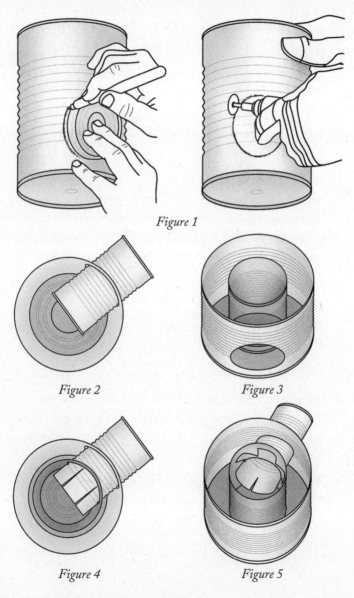

Figure 1

Figure 2

Figure 3

Figure 4

Figure 5

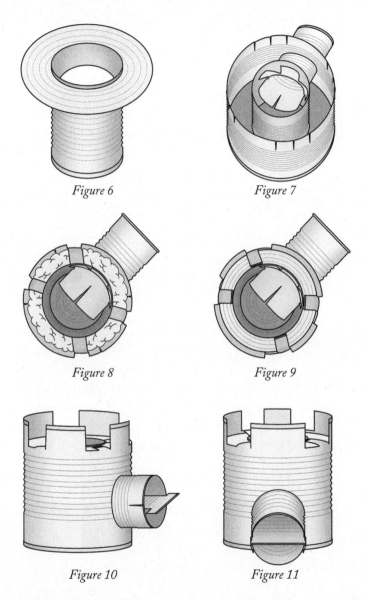

Figure 6

Figure 7

Figure 8

Figure 9

Figure 10

Figure 11

Shelter and Comfort

117

9. Fold down four of the scored tabs (see Figure 9). Place the outer circle you just cut out in step 4 as a cover. Bend down the rest of the scored tabs to secure.

10. Make a shelf for the outer 28-ounce can opening. Using one of the scrap pieces, cut a rectangular piece of metal with flaps that will fit inside. Hammer down to flatten if necessary. (See Figure 10.)

11. Cut 1 inch on either side of the opening of the outer 28-ounce can. Slide the shelf into the opening and bend the side flaps down to secure. (See Figure 11.)

12. Make a handle for the stove. Drill two small holes on either side of the large #10 can. Unbend the wire hanger. Using the wire, shape a handle and bend it into place.

13. Optional: You can paint your rocket stove with heat-resistant spray paint or use it as is. Painting it will make it last longer.

To use the DIY rocket stove, place small pieces of wood, twigs, leaves, fire starter (such as dryer lint), etc., on the top shelf of the outside hole. Light it. Set the pot you are cooking with on top of the stove. Continue to feed it with wood, twigs, or weeds until you finish cooking.

Source: Jamie Black Smith, Prepared Housewives, http://prepared-housewives.com/how-to-build-a-rocket-stove-and-impress-the-boys

How to Make a Fireless Cooker

A fireless cooker, or haybox, was commonly used in the early 1900s to cook food all day in an insulated container. Back then, some commonly used insulating materials included finely cut hay, straw, sawdust, or wool. You might say it was a forerunner of the Crock-Pot, but without electricity.

The fireless cooker cooks food that has been brought to a full boil. While the food is still boiling, you will place the pot inside a box and cover the pot with insulating material. Leave the pot inside for 4 to 8 hours to cook. The food continues cooking for hours at high temperature until you open the box.

These days, you can actually use many types of insulating materials, such as old pillows, material from comforters, styrofoam, shredded paper, wool sweaters, etc.

Why would you use one?

- To conserve fuel in your backup stove. During a power outage, use a backup stove to heat the food to boiling, then leave the boiling pot in a haybox to continue cooking. Cooking in a haybox does not release the smells of cooking food that may invite attention in a down-grid emergency.

- To save energy, money, and time. In normal times, you can cook in food in the morning and have dinner waiting for you at night, all without leaving any appliances on.

EASY FIRELESS COOKER

You will need:

old ice chest (must be large enough to hold your cooking pot)

2 to 3 old, crib-sized comforters or old comforters cut to 41 x 48 inches, edges stitched

foam pillows

Directions:

1. Line the bottom of the ice chest with the comforters and make room for your pot in the middle of the ice chest.

2. Mix your favorite soup ingredients in the pot and bring it to a full boil. Any dishes that involve boiling or steaming, such as soups or stews, would work well.

3. Place the pot in the middle of the ice chest. Line the sides and the top with additional comforters. If using foam pillows, fit the pillows around the pot snugly. Make sure the entire pot is well covered. Cover the top of the pot as well, leaving space to close the ice chest.

4. Leave it alone for 4 to 8 hours, depending on the ingredients you are using. Use oven mitts to lift out the pot as it will still be hot.

ENTERTAINMENT

Entertainment supplies aren't essential, but good for morale. If you've ever been stuck in the house during an emergency, you know it can get boring without power, TV, video games, the Internet, or all the usual entertainment sources, especially if you have kids.

Collect low-tech entertainment options such as:

- arts and crafts
- board games
- books
- drawing materials
- mini tents and blankets so you can build a fort
- music
- puzzles
- writing supplies

Consider what you can use for traditional pastimes like telling scary stories, recounting old family history, playing pretend, or even holding a family talent show. Most of the items on the list above are free or low cost and can be found at garage sales, thrift stores, or bargain bins at discount retailers. Pick these items up and store them in a space that is easily located in the dark. Keeping everyone occupied during a stressful time will help you get through the difficulties smoothly.

Chapter 5

FIRST AID

Even if a disaster were never to occur, every home needs a basic first aid kit. Before going out to buy your first aid supplies, take inventory of what you have right now. Check expiration dates; if most of your supplies expired in the '90s, it is time to toss and replace. Hanging on to old items gives you a false sense of security until you really need them and find out they are useless.

WHAT TO INCLUDE IN FIRST AID KIT

Pain relief. Stock up on acetaminophen (Tylenol or generic) as well as ibuprofen (Motrin or generic) as appropriate for the ages of your family members. Aspirin is also a great pain reliever, but is not recommended for children under 18 years of age as it is said to be related to Reye's syndrome.

Stomach remedies. Include Pepto-Bismol, Imodium A-D, ipecac (to induce vomiting in case of ingesting a poisonous substance), charcoal tablets, and Gatorade or a homemade electrolyte solution (page 126).

Allergy relief. Common products include Diphendydramine (Benadryl), loratadine (Claritin), and cetirizine (Zyrtec).

Basic wound care. Keep sterile gauze and adhesive bandages in assorted sizes, elastic bandages, butterfly bandages, wound tape, antibiotic ointment (Neosporin), hydrogen peroxide, and iodine.

Eye care. Keep saline solution, eye drops such as Visine, reading glasses, extra prescription glasses, and contact lenses (if you have family members who wear them).

Foot care. Moleskin pads for foot blisters, Epsom salts, nail scissors, nail clippers, and a nail fungus remedy (see homemade version on page 127) may all come in handy.

Skin care. Burn cream, aloe vera gel for sunburns, calamine lotion for itches and rashes, hydrocortisone cream (Cortaid).

Dental supplies. Dental supplies include dental floss, mouthwash, oral anesthetic such as Orajel or Anbesol, white filling cement (to reattach crowns or to use as temporary filling), mouthwash, clove oil (to relief toothache pain for adults: to use, apply directly on painful tooth with a Q-tip, then spit out), denture repair kit, dental wax for braces, toothpicks, cotton balls, and Q-tips.

Protective gear. Keep one to two boxes of vinyl medical gloves and facial masks on hand.

Disinfecting solutions. Keep alcohol, antibacterial gel and wipes, and household bleach.

Other first aid supplies:

- blood pressure cuff
- bulb syringe
- first aid manual
- flashlight with extra batteries
- tampons, sanitary napkins
- thermometers (oral and rectal)
- tourniquets
- tweezers
- safety pins
- scissors
- splints
- syringe

Consider your family's overall health needs when stocking your first aid kit. Include extra medications for individual needs, such as birth control pills, prescription medications and supplies for diabetes, high blood pressure medicines, statins, and asthma inhalers and treatments, depending on your family's health needs.

The first aid kit is not a substitute for obtaining proper medical care. You may have to rely on your first aid supplies to tide you over in the event of a disaster when you're unable to drive to the emergency department of the local hospital.

MINI FIRST AID KITS

Create mini first aid kits for your car, office, and purse. Use a coin purse, mint tin, or any recycled mini container, such as a cell phone case, camera pouch, etc. Include:

- adhesive bandages of varying sizes
- allergy/sinus medicine
- antibiotic ointment
- antidiarrheal medicine
- antiseptic wipes
- eye drops
- pain reliever

Money-Saving Ideas for Building Your First Aid Kits

- Join forces with another family or two and split costs for supplies at a warehouse club or big-box store.

- Join email lists to obtain free samples. Many companies offer free trial sizes in exchange for receiving email updates or completing surveys.

- Whenever you visit your doctor, ask for free samples, especially if they are changing your prescriptions.

- Many prescriptions cost the same per pill, regardless of the dosage. Discuss obtaining a higher-dosage prescription with your doctor, and use a pill cutter to cut the pills according to your dosage amount. Do not use a knife to cut the pills, as the dosage may become uneven. If a drug is approved by the FDA for pill splitting, it will be indicated on the package insert. Some pills, such as capsules, are not suitable for splitting. For best results, ask you pharmacist for instructions before splitting pills.

- You can get a lot of freebies at health fairs, conventions, or even at company-sponsored charity events such as

5k runs, walk-a-thons, etc. If you are a participant in an event, the sponsors are happy to give out free stuff.

- Take advantage of offers to transfer prescription drugs. Before ordering a prescription, check the Sunday newspaper inserts for offers for new or transferred prescriptions. Grocery store pharmacies have been known to offer a gift card for new or transferred prescriptions. You can then use the gift card you earned to buy first aid and emergency supplies.

- Learn about the first aid uses for common household items (page 129).

- Learn how to make the home remedies and solutions below.

HOMEMADE ELECTROLYTE SOLUTION

You will need:

8 teaspoons sugar

1 teaspoon salt

1 packet of flavored drink mix

Directions:

1. Combine your ingredients in a sealable plastic bag. Store the dry mix in your first aid kit.

2. When ready to use, mix the dry ingredients with 5 cups of water and stir well. Sip slowly.

NAIL FUNGUS REMEDY

You will need:

one part vinegar   two parts water

Directions:

1. Mix the ingredients. Soak the infected nail in the vinegar/water mixture for 10 minutes, twice per day. Continue the twice-daily soak until the fungus clears up.

ICE PACK

Here are three easy ways to make an ice pack.

Dishwashing liquid. Place 8 ounces of dishwashing liquid into a resealable plastic sandwich bag. Double bag to avoid leaks. Label and place in the freezer for several hours.

Alcohol. In a resealable sandwich bag, combine 1½ cups of water with ½ cup of rubbing alcohol or vodka. Double bag to avoid leaks. Label and place the bag in your freezer for several hours.

Salt. Mix 2 tablespoons of salt with 2 cups of water. Place the mixture in a resealable sandwich bag. Double bag to avoid leaks. Label and place the bag in your freezer for several hours.

HOT PACK

You will need:

old tube sock

needle

1 to 2 cups rice

thread

Directions:

1. Fill the sock with the rice. The amount with depend on the sock size.

2. Sew across the opening or just knot the end.

3. When you need a heating pad for muscle aches or soreness, warm the rice bag in the microwave for 60 seconds and apply. This can also be used as a hand or foot warmer.

NASAL SALINE SPRAY

You will need:

1 teaspoon non-iodized table salt

1 cup distilled water

pinch of baking soda

Directions:

1. Mix all of the ingredients together.

2. Pour the mixture into a sterile nose spray bottle or bulb syringe.

3. Squirt into each nostril three times to relieve dry nasal passages. Use the mixture within a week and make a fresh batch each time you need it.

First Aid Uses of Common Household Items

Sanitary napkins and tampons. The individually wrapped sanitary napkins and tampons are actually good to keep in a first aid kit. US Army medics have been known to use tampons as emergency wound care dressings.

Elmer's Glue or Shoe Goo. These types of glues can be used to remove a sliver. Place a drop over the sliver and let it dry. Once it is dry, pry it off and the sliver should come off with it.

Super Glue. For a minor wound, super glue can be used to seal a cut. Clean the wound and spread a thin layer of super glue on the cut, being careful NOT to get any glue inside the wound. It can cause some skin irritation. (Note: The glue manufacturers do not recommend this use for their product, as there are medical versions available. But we're talking about when there is nothing else around and no medical help is available. Do your own research and use your best judgment).

Duct tape. Duct tape can be used to care for blisters: Cover the blister with gauze, then cover it with duct tape. Don't let the duct tape touch the blister, just the gauze. You can also wrap duct tape around a sprained ankle to give it some support. If you have a cut and no adhesive bandages, use duct tape over clean gauze (or use that sanitary napkin or tampon) to secure it in place. Just don't place the duct tape directly over the wound.

Non-sudsing ammonia. A half-water, half-ammonia mixture can be used to relieve insect bites

Liquid dish soap. Use this with some water to clean cuts.

Credit card, driver's license, or other hard plastic cards. You can use a card to remove a bee's stinger: Scrape across the skin toward the tip of the stinger; this way it comes out the way it came in. Rinse with water.

Wooden ruler. Use this as a splint by wrapping around the injured area with a scarf, belt or bandanna.

Honey. Honey has many first aid uses. Use it as a remedy for burns by spreading it directly on the burn and cover with a soft cloth or gauze. Honey is also used to disinfect wounds and ease a sore throat.

Oatmeal. An oatmeal bath can ease skin rashes from poison ivy and other skin irritations from chicken pox, sun burn or eczema. Place oatmeal in a fine mesh bag or cutup pantyhose and seal, place in a tub and fill with warm water. Soak in the oatmeal bath, and run the bag of oatmeal across the irritated area for some relief.

Vodka. Vodka, due to its alcohol content, makes a great disinfecting solution for hands, needles and surfaces in an emergency. It can also be used to wash small cuts and insect bites. You can gargle with a mixture of half vodka and half water if you feel a sore throat coming on. Swish it around and gargle for 30 seconds then spit it out.

Tea bags. Tea can be used to relieve an upset stomach, especially chamomile, mint, or ginger tea. Black tea bags can be used as an anti-inflammatory solution to soothe skin rashes, insect stings, or hives.

Chapter 6

HYGIENE AND PERSONAL CARE

Every time an emergency is predicted to occur, long lines are guaranteed at grocery and big-box stores and shelves quickly run out of supplies. Hygiene items, such as toilet paper, soap, and feminine products, disappear quickly. Indeed, the day before I experienced my first hurricane in Houston, I myself was in a long, unruly line at the grocery store after I grabbed the last 24-pack of toilet paper from the shelf. I swore I would never again find myself in such a scene and started my emergency preparedness journey soon after the floodwaters cleared.

Preparedness in the hygiene and personal care area is a large component of being prepared for emergencies. Whether an emergency happens or not, we all need to maintain personal cleanliness and maintain our homes. Being prepared with supplies will help you avoid last-minute, late-night trips to the store because you just found out someone used the last roll of toilet paper or your detergent just ran out and you need to wash your child's sports uniform.

Gather your hygiene and cleaning supplies. Stocking up before any emergency happens allows you to clip coupons and combine them with weekly sales at supermarket and discount stores.

What items do you use every day?

Personal Care

- antibacterial gel
- deodorant
- diapers/pull-ups if you have young children
- lotion
- moisturizer
- mouthwash
- razors
- sanitary napkins/ tampons
- shampoo/conditioner (a shampoo/conditioner combo works well and saves money)
- soap or body wash
- toilet paper
- toothpaste

Cleaning

- all-purpose antibacterial spray cleaner
- bleach
- detergent
- dishwashing liquid
- paper towels

Gather at least a month's worth of supplies and store them in 5-gallon buckets. Label the bucket "Hygiene/Personal

Care." The good news is you do not need to wait for an actual emergency to dip into your stores. If you happen to run out of something in the middle of the week, use some of your supply and just replace it as soon as you get restocked. By rotating your products, you keep your stock fresh.

How long do personal care products last? Many personal care products have expiration dates, but they rarely go bad as soon as that date is reached. As they deteriorate, many products may separate, lose their potency or fragrance, or even smell odd. Toothpaste can dry out. Deodorants get hard and crumbly. They don't all go bad at the same time, but over a few years after their expiration date, they lose quality.

In the latter part of this chapter we will discuss alternatives to commonly used personal care products and help you save even more cash.

What is the best way to store toilet paper? Toilet paper rolls are lightweight but occupy a lot of space. To reduce their space requirement, remove the middle cardboard insert and flatten the rolls. Store them in buckets, large zip-top bags, or space bags (remove excess air to flatten them even more).

What do you do if toilets don't work? If the water and sewer system were to go down, you will not be able to flush the toilet. Flushing the toilet may cause waste to overflow into your bathroom. Here are a few options to make an emergency toilet.

Option 1: Make your own temporary toilet. You will need the following materials:

- 1 (5-gallon) bucket with lid
- old toilet seat or two pieces of wood

To use, place the toilet seat or wood pieces parallel across each other to form a seat. You many also purchase a 5-gallon bucket fitted with a plastic toilet seat. They cost around $20 and are available at many online stores or emergency/survival supply stores. Additional supplies include:

- box of 100 heavy-duty trash bags
- cat litter, sand, or sawdust
- baking soda

You may want two separate buckets: one for liquid and one for solid waste.

Line the solid waste bucket with two heavy duty trash bags. Pour a small amount of cat litter each time the toilet is used. Use baking soda to neutralize odor.

If there is no water running, keep hand sanitizer gel nearby to clean hands after using the toilet.

Option 2: Cover your toilet.

Empty the water out of your toilet. Line the toilet bowl with a heavy-duty trash bag. Fit the plastic properly and use duct tape to secure the sides.

Keep these makeshift toilet supplies close to your toilet paper and hygiene supplies.

TOILET PAPER ALTERNATIVES

I'd always wondered what people used before toilet paper was developed. It was interesting to find out how people got by "in the old days."

In ancient times, the Greeks used pieces of clay or stones to clean themselves. The Romans used a softer method: a sea sponge mounted on a stick. After use, they rinsed the sponge and left it soaking in urns filled saltwater.

In colonial times, people used corncobs. Later, they used newspapers and left store catalogs hanging in outhouses.

In some countries, using the left hand to clean oneself while pouring water with the right hand is the method of choice, leading to the left hand being known as the "unclean hand."

If you are in an extended emergency, you may want to conserve your toilet paper supply by using alternatives.

Here are a few ideas:

Baby wipes. As with toilet paper, a large stockpile would have to be accumulated.

Paper substitutes. Newspaper can be used, but the ink would turn everything black. Some people may prefer phone directories, but these days, paper phone books are not as common. Store catalogs may be more available. Just tear the pages, crumple up the sheet until it softens, then wipe.

Cloth. Cloth, such as washcloths, terry cloths, old T-shirts, or cloth diapers, is a good toilet paper substitute. Just cut large pieces into squares. Hem the edges so they don't fray. To use, wet the cloth, wipe, then soak it in water with a small amount of bleach until you are ready to wash them. In fact, some households have opted out of toilet paper completely by using these reusable cloths, as they are economical and environmentally friendly.

Plant material. A couple of options that would work are sage leaves and banana leaves. If you rely on this method, you must have some knowledge about which plants are safe. Avoid poison ivy, poison oak, or sumac—these can really hurt! Remember: *Leaves of three—let it be!*

Water. Use a water carrier, such as the following:

- Small can, like an empty coffee can.
- Spray bottle.
- Perineal irrigation bottle. Usually given to women for use after childbirth, these have a nozzle with three to four holes to aim the water.
- Recycled bottle with a nozzle, such as a dishwashing liquid bottle.

Fill any of these containers with plain water, add a drop of essential oil for fragrance if you like, and wash up. After washing, dry the area with a clean towel that can also be reused.

STAYING CLEAN WHEN WATER IS SCARCE

In an emergency, if the municipal tap water system were to go down, taking a daily shower would not be possible. Here are a few tips to stay clean:

- If the emergency is predictable, such as a hurricane or ice storm, have everyone in the family take a shower before the predicted emergency comes.

- Similarly, finish doing your laundry so you have a supply of clean clothes.

- Fill the tub with water using a tub water collection system, such as the WaterBOB. Or, plug the drain, line the tub with plastic sheeting, and fill it up. This water can be used for washing.

- Stock up on baby wipes, which can be used to clean the face and body.

- Take sponge baths. Switch to using a washcloth moistened with a small amount of water in lieu of a shower.

- To heat water, use a "camp shower," which is a transparent water canister that can be hung on a branch or pole to allow the sun to warm the water.

AVOIDING GERMS

Whether you are just trying to avoid seasonal flus and colds or are concerned about antibiotic-resistant germs such as MRSA, these worries boil down to the basic idea of avoiding germs and keeping your immune system strong. Avoid catching and spreading germs with the following tips:

Isolation. If anyone gets sick, avoid direct contact as much as possible. If possible, sleep in a separate room. Avoid hugging or kissing. If a baby or small child is sick, contact is unavoidable; all you can do is minimize getting coughed on.

Wear gloves and a face mask. Germs are spread by contact with the virus, whether they're in the air or on surfaces the sick person has touched. Flu viruses live on surfaces for 2 to 8 hours. If you wear gloves and a face mask, you will avoid spreading germs all over the house.

Stay home. Sick kids should stay home from school, and sick parents should stay home from work and get some rest. I've learned that trying to power through a bout of the cold and flu just makes you get worse and possibly suffer complications, such as bronchitis or pneumonia, causing more missed days. Getting a day of rest helps you recover faster, thereby avoiding further spread of germs.

Disinfect all commonly used surfaces around the house. Wipe down light switches, TV remotes, doorknobs, refrigerator handles, faucets, and toilet and bathroom fixtures using commercially available disinfecting wipes or your own disinfecting solution such as the one on page 153.

Cover your mouth with a tissue or handkerchief when you cough or sneeze. Immediately dispose of the tissue or wash the handkerchief. If you do not have either, turn away from everyone and sneeze or cough into the crook of your elbow or shoulder.

Stock up. Before you catch a cold or flu, stock up on over-the-counter medications to help relieve symptoms. This way, you avoid having to go out while you're sick.

Change into indoor clothes. After being outside, immediately change out of your clothes and remove your shoes. Your clothes and shoes may have been contaminated and wearing clothes and shoes for indoor use helps avoid the spread of germs.

Avoid taking leftover antibiotics if you don't know what you have. Overusing antibiotics contributes to the spread of drug-resistant germs.

Wash your own hands frequently with soap and water. To thoroughly clean your hands, you must lather up for 20 seconds (sing "Happy Birthday" twice). Get your entire family into the habit of frequent hand-washing. If possible, avoid overusing antibacterial gels and soaps, as they may also contribute to drug-resistant bacteria. Save your antibacterial gels or alcohol-based hand sanitizers for emergencies when water is scarce.

Strengthen your immune system. Get enough sleep and rest. Relax and avoid stress. Exercise at least 3 to 4 days a week. Eat a healthy diet. Take vitamin supplements if you feel you don't eat well enough.

HOW TO MAKE COMMON PERSONAL CARE PRODUCTS AT HOME

A couple years ago, if anyone told me I would be making my own deodorant or moisturizer at home, I'd have said they were crazy. I never would have thought I could do it myself and always relied on store-bought products. As I became more interested in taking steps to be prepared and more self-sufficient, I researched alternatives to products that I can make myself. Knowing how to make product substitutes help you save both time and money. You are also using more natural alternatives so you are not putting as many chemicals and preservatives in your body.

I'm not saying you should replace all your products with homemade alternatives. Knowing how to make substitutes will help you get by in an emergency when you are not able to make a trip to the store.

Just try some of the recipes that interest you and you may be pleasantly surprised. If not, you can always go back to your favorite brands.

Shampoo

In an emergency, if you do not have shampoo, you can use baking soda and apple cider vinegar to clean your hair.

SHAMPOO SUBSTITUTE

You will need:

baking soda   ¼ cup apple cider vinegar

water

Directions:

1. Make a paste using one part baking soda to three parts water, and rub it all over your hair and scalp. The mixture will get rid of oils and buildup.

2. You must follow this by rinsing with ¼ cup apple cider vinegar mixed with 1 cup of water to balance it out. Otherwise your hair will become dry and frizzy.

You can also wash your hair using a bar of soap or a small amount of dishwashing liquid if you do not have baking soda and apple cider vinegar. Though this may not result in shiny, manageable hair, at least your hair and scalp will be clean.

How long can you go without shampoo? I used to wash my hair daily with shampoo, followed by hair conditioner. I then noticed my hair started to feel dry and lifeless. I tried various shampoo brands, and nothing helped. My regular salon advised me to use other, more expensive products to correct the problem, but they did not work. I went to a different hair stylist who told me I was overusing shampoo. She said I should just rinse my hair in the shower, without using shampoo, and only use shampoo once or twice a week at the most. This also eliminated the need for hair conditioner.

The advice seemed strange to me but I tried it. My hair started looking and feeling healthy again. The point is, we may all be overusing hair products and not know it, resulting in hair problems that are easily fixed. Try cutting back your shampoo and hair product usage; you might find that both your hair and your pocketbook will be grateful.

Toothpaste

If you are in an emergency and are out of toothpaste, brush your teeth with plain baking soda. For a minty flavor, use the following recipe.

TOOTHPASTE SUBSTITUTE

You will need:

3 drops peppermint essential oil

1 cup of baking soda

Directions:

1. Mix the ingredients well. Use them to brush and rinse with water.

Mouthwash

Essential oils are oils extracted from plants. They contain fragrance and some have therapeutic properties. This homemade mouthwash uses peppermint essential oil.

HOMEMADE MOUTHWASH

You will need:

- 1 cup distilled water
- 1 teaspoon baking soda
- 3 to 4 drops peppermint essential oil

Directions:

1. Mix the above ingredients in a small bottle.

BENEFITS OF PEPPERMINT ESSENTIAL OIL

Peppermint oil, derived from the leaves, stems and flowers of the peppermint plant, is known for its therapeutic properties. It destroys harmful microorganisms, and is antifungal and antibacterial. Because of its antiseptic properties, it is commonly used as an ingredient for toothpastes and mouthwash. The aroma is energizing and stimulating. One whiff of peppermint oil will make you feel more alert and perky.

Another great use is its insect repellent properties. Peppermint repels many household pests such as ants, mosquitos, cockroaches, and spiders.

Deodorant

You can use cornstarch or baking soda straight out of the box as a deodorant. Use a powder puff or a large brush and lightly brush your underarms.

Plain rubbing alcohol on a cotton ball can also quickly get rid of underarm odors. Do not use on recently shaved armpits, as this will sting!

CREAM DEODORANT

You will need:

¼ cup cornstarch	6 tablespoons coconut oil
¼ cup baking soda	3 to 4 drops lavender oil (optional)

Directions:

1. Mix the cornstarch and baking soda in a bowl.

2. Add the coconut oil and mix with a fork until well blended.

3. Add lavender oil if desired. Store in an airtight container.

SPRAY-ON DEODORANT

As with all products applied to the skin, test the following on a small area before using. Do not use on irritated or broken skin.

You will need:

1 cup purified water

¼ cup witch hazel

1 tablespoon baking soda

3 to 4 drops tea tree essential oil

Directions:

1. Mix the water, witch hazel, and baking soda in a small bowl.

2. Add the tea tree oil and mix well. Pour the mixture into a small spray bottle.

Other Products

REFRESHING FOOT SPRAY

You will need:

1 cup water

¼ cup vodka

10 drops peppermint essential oil

Directions:

1. Mix all ingredients and pour into a spray bottle.

2. Spray on hot, tired feet for soothing relief, or use to control foot odor.

MOISTURIZING SALVE

You will need:

cooking pot large enough to boil water and accommodate the cup

5 tablespoons organic beeswax pastilles

1 cup coconut oil

1 cup pure olive oil

large measuring cup

labels

permanent marker

8 empty 2-ounce recycled or new jars, or small mason jars

your choice of tea tree, eucalyptus, lavender, rosemary, or peppermint essential oil (optional)

Directions:

1. Add water to the pot, and set it on stove to simmer. Add the organic beeswax pastilles, coconut oil, and olive oil to the large measuring cup. Place the measuring cup in the pot.

2. Leave the measuring cup in the pot until the ingredients start to melt. Stir it every once in a while. This will take around 20 minutes. Start labeling your jars with the essential oil used while you are waiting for the oils to dissolve.

3. Leave out the essential oils for unscented moisturizer or makeup remover. Check the simmering pot to see if the ingredients are completely dissolved. If so, you can start pouring the liquefied oils into the jars. Warning:

The glass cup will be extremely hot, so use an oven mitt and carefully pour the melted oils into the jars.

4. Leave the jars uncovered overnight. Find something to cover the uncapped jars, such as paper towels or cloth. The salve may solidify in an hour, but you should leave them alone overnight.

5. Check the jars the next day and your plain moisturizer is ready to use. To create a scented salve, you can add your favorite essential oil or a combination of oils to each jar. Some examples:

   • 5 drops peppermint and 5 drops tea tree oil make a great hand and foot lotion (do not use near your eyes if you add these essential oils).

   • 5 drops lavender and 5 drops eucalyptus are both soothing scents and can also be used separately or together for moisturizers and lip balms.

6. Either melt the salve in the microwave then add the oil or simply add the oils directly to the hardened salve and stir rapidly to mix well.

Source: Gaye Levy, *Simple Salve Backdoor Survival*, http://www.backdoorsurvival.com/diy-all-natural-simple-salve

LIQUID HAND SOAP

You will need:

1 (4-ounce) bar soap	12½ cups water

2 tablespoons glycerin (sold
in the personal care aisle
of pharmacies and grocery
stores)

large pot

large funnel

large empty jug

cheese grater

liquid soap dispenser

Directions:

1. Using the cheese grater, grate the bar of soap.

2. In the large pot, boil the water.

3. Add the grated soap to the pot and stir well.

4. Add the glycerin.

5. Continue boiling until the soap melts. The water will be somewhat clear with some bubbles.

6. Let stand overnight. If your mixture appears to be too thick, just add more water until you like the consistency for liquid soap.

7. Do this step over the sink: Using the large funnel, pour the liquid soap into a large empty jug (such as a clean, 1-gallon milk jug) for storage. The liquid tends to pour in large quantities, so do it very slowly.

8. Now you can pour the liquid soap into your soap dispenser. For maximum savings, use recycled containers.

HOMEMADE BABY WIPES

You will need:

2 cups water

2 tablespoons coconut or olive oil

2 tablespoons baby wash

small pot

roll of paper towels (a strong towel like Bounty works well)

recycled wipes container or plastic container with lid

Directions:

1. Boil the water in a small pot. Add the oil and allow to cool.

2. Add the baby wash to the water.

3. Cut the paper towel roll in half down the middle of the roll. You will be using the first half of the two rolls.

4. Pour the mixture into the plastic container.

5. Place the ½ paper towel roll in the container.

6. Seal and shake to until the paper towels moisten.

7. Remove the cardboard tube from the paper towel roll and pull from the inside so that the towels pull out like wipes.

8. Since this has no preservatives, use within 1 to 2 weeks.

Chapter 7

CLEANING

In an emergency, keeping your space clean and hygienic is very important, both for morale and health reasons. If you like certain cleaning products you can certainly stock up with a bottle or two. In case you run out, the most economical way to go is to learn how to make homemade substitutes.

INSTANT MONEY TIP

Conserve your cleaning and hygiene supplies by using half the recommended amount every time. When using your dishwasher or washing machine, don't fill up the detergent compartments to the brim. Instead, measure half what the manufacturer recommends. I have successfully cut our usage in half by following this tip, thereby doubling the number of uses for each product.

DIY CLEANING PRODUCTS

There are many do-it-yourself formulas available, but it takes quite a bit of trial and error to get ones that work. I have been experimenting with homemade cleaning products for a while and these are the recipes that have been most successful.

Cleaners

NATURAL ALL-PURPOSE CLEANER

You will need:

1 cup citrus rinds (orange, lemon, grapefruit, or a combination)

1 cup white vinegar

recycled 12-ounce jar or mason jar

Directions:

1. Add the white vinegar to a jar.

2. Tear or chop the citrus rinds into nickel-sized pieces and add them to the vinegar, squeezing as you do to release the oils.

3. Store the jar in a cool dark place for 2 to 4 weeks.

4. Strain the peels and pour the solution into a spray bottle. Use it as an all-purpose cleaner and to cut grease and freshen counters. The citrus cuts down on the vinegar smell, which is only temporary.

SCOURING POWDER

You will need:

½ cup baking soda

½ cup salt

½ cup borax

Directions:

1. In a bowl, mix all ingredients together with a fork. Crush any lumps.

2. Pour into a used Parmesan cheese canister if available, or in a jar.

DISINFECTING CLEANER

For several years, Clorox Regular-Bleach contained 5.25 to 6 percent sodium hypochlorite, the active ingredient in bleach. These days, Clorox Regular-Bleach contains a concentration of 8.25 percent sodium hypochlorite, making it more concentrated. However, some brands still come with the old concentrations.

If you are using a different brand of liquid bleach, read the label to find out the level of concentration.

The following mixtures are appropriate for disinfecting surfaces to help combat germs.

You will need:

If using the 8.25% bleach concentration:

¾ teaspoon bleach   2 cups water

If using the 5.25 to 6% bleach concentration:

1¾ teaspoon bleach   2 cups water

Directions:

1. Mix the water with the appropriate measurement of bleach.

2. Add to a spray bottle.

3. Clean the surface with soap and water to get rid of dirt or grime. Spray the area with the bleach solution and leave the solution on the surface for 2 minutes to disinfect. Wipe with paper towels or clean rags to dry.

Note: Do not spray on wood as it may bleach the wood. Do not mix bleach with any other household cleaners such as ammonia or toilet bowl cleaners, as this may result in releasing hazardous gas. For best results, mix a fresh batch daily.

Glass and Window Cleaners

I've tested several homemade glass cleaners with varying results. These two work best for me.

OLD NEWSPAPER

My mom's favorite, old newspaper and water, works very well on mirrors and glass.

Spray the glass with water and scrub with newspaper. It takes a bit of scrubbing, but the result is a streak-free and shiny surface.

ALCOHOL/VINEGAR COMBINATION SPRAY

For those of you who do not have old newspapers lying around, here is an easy-to-mix version with ingredients you likely already have at home.

You will need:

2 cups water

¼ cup white vinegar

¼ cup rubbing alcohol

1 tablespoon cornstarch

8 drops citrus essential oil (optional)

Directions:

Mix all of the ingredients together and add to a spray bottle. The cornstarch may settle in the bottom of the bottle when stored. Just shake the bottle before use to remix.

Air Freshener

There are various low-cost ways to freshen the air in your home without using chemical air fresheners:

Coffee grounds: Place used coffee grounds in a bowl and let them sit out for a day. The coffee grounds will freshen the air. This tip also works to deodorize a smelly fridge. You can discard or throw in the compost after a day or two.

Scented water: Boil water in a pot and throw in orange and lemon rind. Let it simmer for 5 to 10 minutes. You can use a variety of spices and scents, such as cinnamon, cloves, or vanilla, alone or in combination.

HOMEMADE AIR-FRESHENING SPRAY

I like to use eucalyptus oil, which makes the room smell like a spa, and fresh scents such as orange, lemon, or lavender.

You will need:

¾ cup water

¼ cup vodka

10 drops of your favorite essential oil

Directions:

Place all the ingredients together in a spray bottle and mix.

Dishwashing Powder

DISHWASHING POWDER

Borax and washing soda can be found in the laundry aisle of most department stores. Walmart usually carries both at a great price.

You will need:

1 cup borax

1 cup washing soda

¼ cup kosher salt

1 packet of unsweetened, lemon-flavored Kool-Aid

dishwashing liquid

white vinegar

Directions:

1. In an airtight jar, mix the borax, washing soda, and kosher salt. Mix well and blend any lumps. Add the unsweetened, lemon-flavored Kool-Aid packet. Seal the airtight jar to store.

2. To use, place 1 tablespoon of the mixture into your dishwasher's detergent compartment.

3. Add 2 to 3 drops of dishwashing liquid. Add white vinegar to the rinse aid compartment. The last two steps help make your dishes sparkling clean—do not leave these steps out.

Laundry Detergents

DIY LIQUID LAUNDRY DETERGENT

You will need:

8 cups water

3 tablespoons borax

3 tablespoons washing soda

2 tablespoons dishwashing liquid

8 drops lavender or orange essential oil (optional)

¼ cup white vinegar

clean and empty juice container

funnel

Directions:

1. Add the water to the empty container. Using a funnel, add the borax and washing soda to the water. Shake until well mixed. Add the dishwashing liquid and shake some more. If you'd like a fragrance, add 8 drops of lavender or orange essential oil to the mixture.

2. To use, add ¼ cup of the mixture to the detergent compartment of your washing machine.

3. Add white vinegar to the fabric softener compartment. Wash as normal.

DIY POWDER LAUNDRY DETERGENT

Fels-Naptha and ZOTE laundry soap are available in the laundry aisle of discount or grocery stores.

You will need:

1 bar Fels-Naptha or ZOTE laundry soap

1 cup borax

1 cup washing soda

Directions:

1. Grate the bar of Fels-Naptha or ZOTE soap.

2. In a jar, add the grated soap, borax, and washing soda. Mix well. If you want a fine powder, run the ingredients in a blender or food processor.

3. Seal the jar to store. To use, add 1 tablespoon of the homemade detergent to each load and wash as normal.

OFF-GRID LAUNDRY METHODS

Doing laundry without electricity requires more time and energy than simply throwing the clothes in the washing machine, adding soap, then drying in a clothes dryer. In case power were to go out for an extended period, it's good to have a backup plan for washing clothes.

There are a lot of gadgets available to help you do laundry without power. However, because we are trying to spend as little as possible, I will offer the lowest-cost options available.

WASH ONLY WHEN CLOTHES ARE DIRTY

During "normal" times, most people wash according to a schedule rather than evaluating each piece of laundry. They may throw their daily outfits in the dirty clothes pile after wearing once, wash sheets and towels weekly, etc. But if you think about it, most articles of clothing, except for underwear or socks, stay clean even after being worn several times, unless the person works with dirt or trash or gets extremely sweaty every day. In an emergency where water is scarce and power may be interrupted, people would cut back on washing clothes until they are dirty.

Hand and Plunger Methods

Minimum materials you will need:

- 2 (5-gallon) buckets
- rope or paracord to string clotheslines for drying
- clothespins to secure clothes to the clotheslines, and/or plastic hangers to hang clothes
- Store-bought or homemade laundry detergent

THE HAND METHOD

I. Soak the dirty clothes in a 5-gallon bucket of soapy water for a couple of hours. Soaking loosens up dirt and grime. Then, add laundry detergent and simply use your hands to scrub and agitate the clothes to further remove dirt.

2. Rinse the clothes in a second 5-gallon bucket of water until all traces of soap are gone.

PLUNGER METHOD

1. Cut small holes across a brand-new toilet plunger to allow water to pass through.

2. Place three to four articles of clothing in a 5-gallon bucket. Add water to moisten the clothes, add ½ cup of laundry detergent.

3. Use the plunger to agitate the clothes in an up, down, and sideways motion. Rinse as usual.

Stomp on the Clothes

Use the bathtub to wash clothes. Plug the drain and add ½ cup detergent to the water. Start stomping your (clean) feet on the clothes to loosen dirt. Rinse.

Heavily Soiled Clothes

If the clothes are extremely dirty and stained, soaking the clothes in boiling water will help remove stains and sanitize the clothes. Set a large pot of water to boil. Remove from heat and add the dirty clothes. Leave the clothes in the hot water until the water cools then use one of washing methods above.

Wringing Clothes

After hand-washing the clothes, wring them out by hand to remove as much water as possible. You can have another person help you with larger items, such as towels or sheets. Hold one end while the other person holds the other end. Start twisting the clothes until most of the water has been wrung out.

Another way to wring out the water is by using a mop wringer.

Drying Clothes

Hang the clothes outside to dry while the sun is out. Use a hanger or clothespins to secure each piece of clothing to the rope or paracord.

INSTANT STAIN REMOVERS

Use enough to cover the stain:

- Lemon juice whitens clothes and removes oil stains.
- Vinegar and dishwashing detergent remove oily stains.
- Baking soda removes underarm stains.
- Hydrogen peroxide is good for organic stains, such as blood and dirt stains.
- Vodka is effective for ink stains.

Chapter 8

COMMUNICATIONS

One of my biggest fears should an extended emergency happen is being unable to stay informed about what's going on and losing contact with loved ones. To mitigate these fears, I have come up with an emergency communications plan, as well as ways to stay informed when power goes out.

Before an emergency happens, create a family emergency communications plan of your own. This is a quick project that can be done in one weekend. To start, put together a list of emergency contacts.

EMERGENCY CONTACT LIST

It won't cost you anything to collect all of your contacts' information, including:

- name
- address
- phone numbers for work, home, and cell phone
- parents'/children's names and their contact information
- health concerns

- frequently called numbers
- include additional numbers of your business and household contacts, including:
    - doctors
    - dentist
    - day care center or caregiver
    - children's schools
    - work or business contacts such as your boss, business partner, assistant, etc.
    - home, auto, health, and life insurance companies
    - utilities such as electricity, gas, water/sewer, cable/ Internet

Assemble the emergency contact list in a binder. Insert each page into a clear sheet protector to protect it from moisture.

I have an emergency contact binder and it has come in handy in many situations, not just disasters. We had a localized power outage recently and the whole neighborhood lost power. I consulted the binder and called our electric company. I found out a transformer in the area had gone down and the crew was dispatched. When an unusual occurrence like this happens, it is always a relief to find information as quickly as possible.

EMERGENCY COMMUNICATIONS PLAN

Before you can come up with a plan, you need to evaluate your own situation and think about the following considerations:

- How would you deal with a sudden emergency that occurs in the middle of the day, when most family members are at work or school?

- What type of emergency would cause you to drop everything and rush home?

- Who will do school pickups? In areas where tornadoes occur, there is a small window of time when a tornado warning is issued and residents are able to leave and rush to a tornado shelter. Parents can rush home and pick up their children before going to a tornado shelter. You should be aware of the emergency procedures at your office and children's schools.

- Can you get out of your office building if elevators are not working?

These are the nitty-gritty details that you need to find out about as you formulate your emergency plan. The main point of this exercise is to allow you to think ahead on what you would do if your family were in different areas during an emergency.

In a crisis scenario, there may be a remote possibility that you would have to send someone your child's never met to pick them up. We all tell our children never to go with strangers, so there has to be a way to communicate that someone is trustworthy. Come up with code words you can use with small children to establish whom they can trust to pick them up. The code word should be something just you and child would know and remember.

Consider these and the following details to come up with a plan, and discuss the plan with the rest of your family. This way, you won't be running around in a panic and will avoid misunderstandings when an emergency occurs.

Where to Meet

Establish a secondary meeting place if your home is inaccessible for whatever reason. It could be Grandma's house, the coffee shop around the corner, or even the nearest grocery store. As long as it is safe and known to everyone in the family, it can be included as a backup meeting place.

Calling and Texting Trees

This project is simple and free, and can be done in an hour or so. Using your emergency contact list, choose whom you will want to call or text in the event of an emergency, such as an earthquake or hurricane. You can either draw it out manually or build the tree using Word or Excel in the same manner you would create an organizational chart.

Since you are the organizer, place yourself at the top of the tree. You would then call or text three people, who would have another three people to contact, and so on. In a disaster, you have limited cell phone reception, so keep your contacts to a maximum of three. They must be contacts you can count on to get the word out.

Call the friends and family members who are on your list and explain how the calling and texting tree works. Give them the choice of whom to call or text. Even non-preppers in your circle would see the need to be able to communicate in the event of an emergency, so it should be fairly easy get them on board.

STAYING CONNECTED

Cable and satellite TV frequently go down during emergencies, leaving people unable to communicate, watch the news, and stay informed about what's going on.

To stay aware, you need to have a few alternate options so you don't feel completely isolated when power or cable/satellite services are down.

Internet

If you still have Internet, you can get your news online. Google has a service called Public Alerts (http://google.org/publicalerts), where you can get local news bulletins such as flood or storm watches by typing in your city and state.

Try communicating with your family and friends via email if necessary.

Social Media

During Hurricane Sandy, many affected residents felt cut off from services until they took to social media and started communicating with others. A lot of updates were received through Twitter and Facebook, and emergency departments in the area monitored these sites for information on pockets of communities that were otherwise isolated.

Cell Phone

Smart phone apps you can use for emergencies:

News and weather. You can download news apps from your local TV and radio stations directly to your phone. You can set up how you want to receive your notifications.

County emergency alerts. Some counties offer emergency alerts as well.

Police scanner apps. Some carriers offer police scanner apps from various areas all over the world. The quality and type of communications you may receive varies greatly; some areas are more informative than others.

Traffic apps. During the 2015 flooding disaster in Houston, hundreds of drivers became stranded due to high water and flash floods. Roads quickly became impassable and many freeways and highways were shut down. Traffic apps will allow you to check which roads to avoid during an emergency and help you plan the safest routes.

Before you download apps, read the terms of service to find out what personal information is being collected from your phone by the app itself.

Some tips on staying connected:

- Keep your phone charged at all times. Make it a habit to charge your phone every night so you don't run the risk of your power going out when something unforeseen occurs.

- During an emergency, conserve your smartphone's power by disabling apps that are unnecessary at the moment. You can always restore them later when the emergency has passed.

- Texting may work even if calling does not.

- Avoid making unnecessary calls.

- Inactive cell phones, as long as they are charged, can be used to dial 911 for emergency use only. Keep one as a backup.

- Carry a backup charger, preferably one that is solar-powered.

Weather Radio

Pick up an inexpensive weather AM/FM radio, preferably with backup power, such as a hand-crank charger or solar. The only transmissions received might be AM radio, but that is better than no news at all. You won't be able to communicate with anyone, but you can pick up information that may impact you.

Indoor HDTV Antenna

An indoor HDTV antenna makes a great backup in case cable or satellite TV goes down. You can get all the free channels and the picture quality is great. This is another option to allow you to find out what's going on around you.

FRS/GMRS Two-Way Radio

We own a few sets of these two-way radios and use them when traveling with other families on road trips. They have a range of around 5 to 35 miles or so (generally), but brands vary widely, so do your research before buying. Some come in pairs or may be available in a three-, four-, or six-pack. They also pick up weather channels and alert systems. They are very affordable, starting at around $25 and up, depending on the features.

What do FRS or GMRS mean? FRS stands for Family Radio Service, and GMRS stands for General Mobile Radio Service. Both function for two-way communications. The main difference is FRS can be used by anyone, while GMRS requires a license to operate. It is important to remember that they operate according to "line of sight," which means that buildings, trees, and other obstructions may interfere with usage. We have found them useful in many situations, so I would encourage you to try them out in various places to see how they work in your area.

CB Radio

CB stands for Citizens' Band radio. According to the Federal Communications Commission (FCC), it is a service for short-range communication intended for use by the general public.

A license is not required to operate one. A CB radio user has access to 40 different channels.

The setup usually consists of a radio, microphone set, and antenna. Usually the antenna is purchased separately from the radio and microphone set. The range is determined by the antenna and other features of the model that you choose and is indirectly affected by weather and terrain.

Radio Scanner

Radio scanners pick up multiple frequencies from two-way radio activity. You cannot transmit, you can only listen. Also known as "police scanners," radio scanners can be used to monitor communications from dispatchers to officers as well as other communications, such as that of fire departments, taxis, air traffic control, ambulances, and mall security. A scanner stops at the first channel it finds with activity and moves on to the next. Users include new media personnel, radio hobbyists, or just average folks who are interested in what's going on in their area. In some instances, police communications may encrypt their broadcasts or go offline to maintain radio silence in certain situations; however, many police departments continue to keep them open and accessible by radio scanners.

Ham Radio

Ham radio, also known as "amateur radio," was established by the FCC as non-commercial, voluntary radio communications service. It is well-known as for emergency backup communications and is often used to find out about severe weather reports from trained "spotters" who voluntarily notify TV and news sources of impending weather emergencies.

Although a license is not required to buy or listen in to ham radio, you need a license to transmit legally through the system.

If you are interested in learning from other ham radio enthusiasts, it is a good idea to join your local ham radio club. You should be licensed prior to joining; however, having equipment is not a requirement. A ham radio club has equipment that you can get familiar with and practice on under the supervision of a licensed operator.

Equipment costs can add up, and it is best to get some expert advice before buying. If you find that you'd like to get more involved with ham radio, you will be more likely to find contacts who can help you find and set up used ham radio equipment.

Neighbors

Neighbors may have to rely on each other in the event of a disaster. Take the time to get to know your neighbors before a disaster occurs. In the aftermath of Hurricane Ike, many neighborhoods that were isolated due to flooding and power loss relied on each other by sharing food and generator power. By getting to your neighbors, you will also be able to ascertain whom you can trust. You may find you have neighbors who share your interest in being prepared, and you can help each other not only in emergencies, but during everyday situations as well.

Community Bulletin Boards

If there were a long-term disaster and communications were to break down, people would have to fall back on physical means to communicate.

Before an emergency happens, choose at least three bulletin boards in various areas within walking distance. Discuss them with your family and familiarize yourselves with their locations. Agree to post on these boards if anything happens and you are unable to communicate in other ways.

Chapter 9

SAFETY AND DEFENSE

Protecting yourself and your home from intruders is a crucial part of being prepared. In a disaster situation, thieves and looters may target the unwary, so you need to have your wits about you to stay safe. Predators may prey on those that they perceive as weak. Being prepared includes staying safe and potentially defending yourself should the need arise.

During a large-scale disaster, police, fire, and other safety personnel may not be around to protect citizens. They may be overwhelmed with calls from all over town and unable to respond to everyone needing help. This is when the criminal element, realizing there is no one around to stop them, may take advantage of the situation. Or, people may be desperate enough to try and take food and supplies from others they perceive to have more than they do. We hope never to find ourselves on the receiving end of this situation; however, we must be prepared just in case. At the same time, we also need to keep in mind that rule of law is frequently restored after the emergency. We can all recall images of lawlessness during Hurricane Katrina; they were appalling, but thankfully, the breakdown was temporary and many perpetrators were brought to justice. Our goal is to be safe, during normal times as well as in emergencies, and to do so in the most cost-effective and practical manner.

SITUATIONAL AWARENESS

While walking the dog through our neighborhood, I see many people who are so engrossed in their phones that they don't even look up to cross the street. Others seem to be on autopilot, backing their cars out of driveways without ever looking around to check for other cars or pedestrians. I pay attention to these drivers and wait it out on the corner since I know they cannot see me even though they are looking in my direction. When they do finally notice me, they are startled and practically jump out of their seats since they were so unaware someone was standing there.

There seems to be an epidemic of a lack of awareness these days. Call it mindfulness or situational awareness—it is a skill that can help save your life. Being aware of one's surroundings will give you an early warning if danger is afoot. Danger can be anything from a thief targeting you or a car that can run you over if you are not paying attention.

Wherever you are, take the time to put away your phone and any other distractions. Actively look around and notice your surroundings. When entering a building, notice all the entrances and exits, the people around you, and anything or anyone that feels out of place. I am not saying you are in danger everywhere you go, but if you make it a habit to pay attention even when in safe surroundings, you will develop the skill of situational awareness.

It takes 21 days to make a habit, and if you aren't accustomed to viewing your surroundings, your situational awareness will disappear unless you make it a point to practice it daily.

As soon as you step out of your home or vehicle, look around and pay attention to everything around you. When entering an establishment such as a bank or restaurant, notice who greets you and who is behind the counter. If you have kids, you can teach them this skill without frightening them by making it into a game. Being observant is a great skill anyone can practice and use to their advantage.

ARE YOU TRULY SAFE CLOSE TO HOME?

Insurance statistics indicate that most accidents happen within 5 to 10 miles of home. At the same time, security experts also find many people become crime victims close to their home or a home base, such as a college dorm or hotel. This is likely because people let their guard down when they are in their comfort zones. They may also neglect personal safety precautions, such as locking their doors or even putting on a seatbelt if they feel they are just around the corner from home. Don't become a statistic—take the same safety precautions wherever you are, even if you feel comfortable in your area.

PRACTICE OPERATIONAL SECURITY ("OPSEC")

Operational security is a term that originated in the military. It means making sure adversaries do not find out critical information about you; or, in plain terms, being careful that bad guys don't find out information they can use against you. Remember the old World War II saying "Loose lips sink ships," meaning "Be careful what you say."

This should be practiced during normal times, and especially during a disaster, when you may be even more vulnerable.

What kinds of information can be harmful to you? Any personal information, including banking details, credit standing, employment information, medical information, social security number, hobbies, political leanings, travel destinations, supplies, skills, and even possessions can be critical.

If you've seen the movie *Home Alone*, you may remember the scene near the beginning of the movie when the two thieves pretended to be security guards and asked about Christmas vacation plans in the neighborhood. They were actually casing the neighborhood for their next victims. If everyone didn't speak about their plans so freely, it would not have been as easy to find targets.

How do you practice operational security?

- Before tossing out paper records, make sure they do not contain information about you. Shred anything that may contain identifying information using a cross cut shredder.

- Watch what you say in social media. Do not reveal your daily schedule or places you are about to visit.

- Avoid responding to emails asking for your personal information. Don't click on email links—most legitimate notices from companies advise you to go to their website directly. Keep your preps and supplies private. This is no one else's business. People will either form conclusions, labeling you as paranoid or a "nut," or they will assume you have tons of money because you are buying gear and supplies.

- If you know you will have a lot of strangers in your home, such as during an open house or a neighborhood function, consider moving some of your gear to a trusted friend or relative's home, or a storage facility.

- Be wary of any strangers visiting your home, such as pizza delivery personnel, a plumber, installers, etc. I'm not saying they are all out to get you; just be aware of who is coming and going and keep rooms that they do not need to be in closed.

- Don't leave boxes from large appliances out on the curb. They announce to the entire block you just bought a large, flat-screen TV, a computer, or a year's worth of freeze-dried food. Shred the boxes instead.

HOW TO THINK LIKE A THIEF

Our local news recently reported a rash of SUV tire and rim thefts, and the crime usually happens in a person's driveway sometime during the night. The owner typically finds all four tires gone and faces an expensive bill of several hundred dollars to replace their tires. Thieves often target items which people don't even give a second thought to.

To avoid being a victim of crime, it helps to think like a thief.

Perception

A thief perceives things differently from you and me. Consequently, items that we take for granted on a daily basis may attract their attention. Some examples:

- Moms may carry around heavy purses filled with snacks, coupons, and old receipts, thinking there is nothing anyone would want in there, but a thief notes that the purse looks loaded and therefore may carry lots of goodies.

- A jogger may leave the house to go for a run with nothing but a cell phone and keys thinking he has nothing valuable, but in reality, thieves find that cell phones have a great resale value and therefore target the jogger for his phone.

- You leave a shopping bag full of trash in the back seat of your car, thinking to dump it later, but all a thief sees is the Nordstrom bag full of something and breaks your car window to check it. There was nothing in the bag, but you are still out a car window. This could have been avoided had you removed the bag right away.

The point is, avoid calling attention to yourself or your personal belongings by minimizing items that may call a thief's attention to you.

1. Keep your curtains and blinds closed. If you must keep your windows open, position your appliances, computers, and valuables away from view to where thieves can't easily spot them.

2. Park your car in your garage, and close the garage door. If a thief does not see your vehicle, he or she will be less likely to steal it.

3. When out shopping, leave your packages inside the trunk of the car.

4. Avoid wearing expensive or shiny jewelry and watches— they make you an attractive target.

Opportunity

Many crimes are crimes of opportunity. A thief spots an easy way to grab your belongings and takes advantage. Don't make yourself easy to rob.

- When grocery shopping, do not leave your purse in the shopping basket as you peruse the produce. Do not leave your car door unlocked with the keys in the ignition, even though you are just running into the convenience store for less than a minute.

- A distracted person can easily become a victim. As we discussed earlier, situational awareness is the number one rule of personal safety. When going about your day, avoid being overly encumbered by carrying or holding too many things. Have at least one hand free at all times.

HOME ROBBERIES

Many home robberies now occur in the middle of the day, instead of at night. Most people are either at work or at school during the day and criminals know it. Even if you are not home, make it look like someone is home: Keep all doors and windows locked, and keep window coverings closed so they cannot tell who is at home. Leave a radio or TV on.

According to reformed ex-burglars, most home robberies take only 8 to 12 minutes, including the time used to get in and out of your home. The first 1 to 2 minutes are used to break in then move on to the master bedroom in search of cash, jewelry, guns, or anything they can carry out. If the safe is not bolted down, they can easily take it with them. Some experts recommend having a decoy jewelry box, with some nice costume jewelry and $20 to $40 in cash so the thief looks no further.

HOW TO BE THE GRAY MAN

Many prepping sites discuss the concept of being "the gray man" to avoid standing out and being targeted.

In our society, people like to be noticed by wearing the latest fashions, owning trendy items, and generally keeping up with what is "in" at the moment. There is nothing wrong with that, while times are normal. However, being remembered as the prosperous one may not be advantageous in a long-term disaster situation as people may assume you have things that they don't. When even basic needs, such as food, water, shelter, first aid, etc., are not being met, life for those known to be "haves" rather than "have nots" will become increasingly dangerous. Being the gray man means blending into the neighborhood and appearing to be like everyone else to escape notice. For example, if everyone else is unable to cook food, you would not want to have a delicious-smelling barbecue aroma coming out of your house. This will draw hungry hoards from miles around. When you are out and about, dress in plain, unaccented clothes similar to everyone else—looking and smelling good would just call attention to you.

The next stop is usually the bathroom and medicine cabinet in search of prescription drugs or narcotics. The last stop would be the living room, office, or study in search of electronics, laptops, and cameras. Personal computers are highly attractive as they also contain personal financial information. The burglar carrying the loot then gets picked up by an accomplice in a car, and they move on to the next targets.

Now that you know a burglar's usual search pattern, think about where you keep your valuables right now. Do you keep all your jewelry in your jewelry box in the master bedroom? Do you have cash on top of your dresser? Reevaluate where you keep things and start varying your hiding places. Place your items in hard-to-search areas such as a child's room in a filled toy box, tucked in a bookshelf among several books, or in a box with miscellaneous items labeled "Baby clothes for donation" or something completely uninteresting. The only caveat about spreading out your valuables is to keep track of all your hiding places or you may forget and end up donating or throwing them in the trash. We've all heard those stories that have gone viral where the owner accidentally sells a priceless engagement ring that they left inside another item in a garage sale—don't let this happen to you.

HOME INVASIONS

In many big cities and towns, home invasion robberies are happening with increasing frequency. In many instances, criminals knock on the door and force their way in as soon as someone opens the door. They then terrorize the home's occupants to find out where the valuables are and take off with the victim's car. Home invasions are worse than home robberies as the victims are often seriously hurt or possibly killed.

Should you answer the door when a stranger knocks? Law enforcement personnel recommend that you answer the door without opening it. You can ask what the person wants from behind closed doors. The reason for this is many potential burglars knock on the door to see if anyone is home. If no one answers, they may break in.

Nine times out of ten, the person ringing the doorbell may have a legitimate purpose and there is no reason to fear.

If you have a peephole in the front door or a side window, use it to view who's calling. If you get a bad feeling about the caller outside, trust your gut and do not open the door. Have your phone ready in case you have to call 911.

Teach young children never to open the door when someone knocks or rings the doorbell.

Discuss an escape plan with the adults in the home in case of a break-in while you are at home. Know how to get yourself and your kids to safety. Everyone has a different home layout and only you can determine the best way out. Have your weapon of choice ready and know how to use it in the event of a confrontation. We will be discussing weapon choices later in this chapter.

DO YOU NEED A HOME SECURITY SYSTEM?

Home security systems can be a good component of an overall safety plan. Many burglars either bypass homes with alarm system signs or admit they have unsuccessfully tried to rob homes with monitored alarm systems.

You can either have a monitored or a non-monitored security system. I've tried both.

Having a monitored security system means an outside company such as ADT or even your local cable company connects to your alarm system 24/7 and monitors the activity. A non-monitored system means the alarm will chime but there is no outside connection. A monitored system has a lot of features depending on your budget: video surveillance, carbon monoxide alerts, mobile phone apps, motion sensors, etc.

However, having the best system in the world will not help you if you or your family habitually forgets to set the alarms. Not long ago, there was a well-publicized robbery in one of the affluent neighborhoods in our city. The homeowner was a local socialite and the contents of her home and closet were featured in some fashion sites. Soon after she became well-known, her home was robbed of several valuables. She indicated she did not set the alarm system when she went out to dinner, since the restaurant was very close by.

Before investing in a home alarm system, assess your family's needs and habits honestly. If you do decide your budget can accommodate the extra expense, get all the information you can before signing the contract. Pay attention to details like:

- length of the contract
- what happens if you have to move

- penalties for early termination
- cost of installation and monthly bill
- cost of a maintenance or repair visit after the initial installation
- how to reset passwords
- training on how to use the alarm system
- what happens during a power outage—does the company have a battery backup?

In addition, you should have a plan in mind on what you would do if the alarm were to go off due to an intruder while you are at home. Do you have a room in the house where everyone can run to?

A NOTE ABOUT SECURITY CAMERAS

I have mixed feelings about installing security cameras outside your doors. On one hand, they may give you a feeling of security that you will be able to view any possible intruders remotely. On the other hand, having the security camera itself calls attention to your home if it is uncommon in the neighborhood. Remember our discussion about avoiding unwanted attention by criminals? Having a security camera when no one else does makes a criminal think, "What stuff must they have that is worth a security camera?" However, if nearly everyone in the neighborhood has one, then no one will think twice about it. Just make sure your particular device sends encrypted signals; otherwise, other people may get to see your security videos.

Low-Tech Home Safety Tips

A few years ago, I locked myself out of my house. I was living in a one-story house at the time. I started walking around the house examining every door and window. I found one of the windows had a small opening. All I had to do was find a brick to stand on, remove the window screen, and lift the window. After a few minutes, I was back inside the house. It then occurred to me that if I could find my way in that easily, a burglar could get into the house the same way just as easily. Try this exercise yourself—you may find it eye-opening. Then, take the steps necessary to reinforce weak access points.

SLIDING GLASS DOORS

Sliding glass doors are very easy to wiggle through and break into. You can install key locks on the top and bottom of sliding glass doors. They range in price from about $5 to $8 and are easy to install.

A low-cost way to reinforce a sliding glass door is to place a heavy rod or stick in the bottom tracks of the sliding door. You can purchase a metal rod that is adjustable to the length of your sliding door track. Or, if you prefer the DIY method, use two old broom handles. Use a long broom handled fitted to the size of the track for when it is completely closed, or use the shorter broom handle if you want to leave the slider slightly open.

TREES AND SHRUBBERY

Trim all trees and shrubbery around your home. Overgrown foliage may be used by someone to hide and skulk around your home. Keeping bushes at a maximum height of 3 feet will allow you to have a clear view of everything around your home.

DEAD BOLT LOCKS

Install dead bolt locks with keyed entry from both sides on all your outer doors. Secure the locks' strike plates into the doorframe with long screws. (The strike plate is the metal part covering the hole in the doorframe where the dead bolt enters.) Commonly used screws are only 1 inch long. Replace the 1-inch screws with 3½-inch screws. This will attach the strike plate against the frame more securely.

LOW-COST DIY DEAD BOLT LOCK

You will need:

2 large eye screws	recycled sturdy metal bar, around 8 to 12 inches, depending on your door frame

Directions:

1. Position the 2 large eye screws on two sides of the interior of your door: one on the door itself and the other on the doorframe.

2. Before screwing them on, make sure your metal bar fits inside the screws and can reach across both screws with at least a 3-inch clearance on both sides.

3. Once the screws are fastened, position the metal bar across and keep it centered at all times.

SHOULD YOU GET A DOG?

Burglars hate dogs, large or small, and admit they will bypass homes that are known to have dogs. However, getting a dog is a big responsibility and expense. Dogs need a lot of love and attention—don't get a dog solely for the purpose of guarding your house. If you do not have a dog, or even if you have one, use "Beware of Dog" signs as a deterrent. Even if you don't have one, go as far as having a dog water and feeder outside your back door. There are also "barking dog" alarms that detect movement and trigger an alarm that mimics the sound of a barking dog.

An *alarm dog*, also known as a watch dog, is the type of dog that will warn its owner by barking when something is amiss. They will bark nonstop when they sense an intruder but cannot be expected to step in front of you to protect you or bite the intruder. Any dog, regardless of size, breed, or strength, can be an alarm dog.

A *guard dog* will not only bark, it will bite or attack an intruder. A good guard dog will initially appear aggressive and forceful as a defensive measure; it will not attack unless the threat does not back away. Good guard dog breeds include German shepherds, Doberman pinschers, bullmastiffs, rottweilers, and Staffordshire terriers.

DOOR AND WINDOW ALARMS

Buy inexpensive door and window entry alarms that attach to the doorframe. They make a loud noise if an entry is breached.

SECURITY BARS

A heavy steel security bar wedged against the inside door knob and the floor can help prevent entry from the outside.

TIMERS

Timers are inexpensive, $10 to $12 units that plug into the wall socket. You plug the lamp into the timer and set the time the light should turn on or off.

TV LIGHT SIMULATORS

Rather than leaving the TV on, use these small devices (priced around $25 to $30) to simulate the flickering lights emitted by a TV and make your home look occupied. From the outside, it just looks like someone is home watching HDTV, but the energy used is that of a night-light.

HOW TO STAY SAFE DURING CIVIL UNREST

In recent months, there have been multiple incidents in the news involving peaceful protests turning into violent confrontations. There is no telling what could trigger such an event, but we all know they could rapidly escalate, and innocent bystanders can potentially get caught up and hurt.

If you find yourself in a deteriorating crowd situation, stay calm and resist the urge to panic. Try to leave the area immediately, moving in the same direction as the traffic. Attempting to move against traffic would make it harder and may call unwanted attention to you. Avoid stopping to take pictures or video—it is not worth your life.

Whether you agree or disagree with the protesters, avoid siding with anyone or getting involved in their altercation.

If you are with a group, stay close to one another. If you have children with you, keep a tight hold on them, and carry the smallest child if possible.

If you are in a vehicle, keep all your doors and windows locked. Avoid main streets and take an alternate route home. There will be a lot of people running in different directions, so watch out for pedestrians.

NON-LETHAL WEAPONS

Have you ever been in a situation when you wished you had a way to defend yourself? Perhaps you found yourself alone in a dark alley or felt vulnerable while walking back to your car in a sketchy neighborhood. Owning a firearm is an option that we will discuss later in this chapter. But for people who live in states where firearms are hard to procure or have personal objections about owning a gun, there are other ways to defend oneself without resorting to lethal force.

Pepper Spray

Pepper spray is a defense agent where the main ingredient is the pepper derivative oleorsein capiscum (OC). Pepper spray causes inflammation and a severe burning sensation of the eyes, nose, throat, and skin.

DIFFERENCE BETWEEN MACE AND PEPPER SPRAY

Mace is a chemical irritant that is similar to tear gas. Pepper spray works more quickly than Mace.

Mace does not work on persons who are under the influence of drugs or alcohol, but pepper spray does.

"Mace" is now also a brand name that makes pepper spray products.

TYPES OF PEPPER SPRAYS

Foam. A heavy, thick liquid similar to a shaving cream consistency. It is less likely to be affected by wind. Also, if your attacker tries to wipe it off, he will end up rubbing it deeper into the skin, causing even more irritation and pain.

Stream or broken stream. Much like getting squirted by a water gun, the stream or broken stream will deliver a large amount of pepper spray with a longer range. The downside is, the canister will get used up faster.

Forced cone. This is the most common type that keychain-style pepper sprays emit. The range is about 6 to 12 feet, covering an area roughly the size of a human head. The mist that escapes is finer than what's delivered by a stream canister, but there is some risk of blowback if you are outside on a windy day.

Fogger. This covers a larger area and delivers an even finer mist than forced cone. It is good for crowd control and protection from bears. Because it is like a mini fire extinguisher, releasing a large amount of spray, there is some risk of blowback, but the attacker will go down even in windy conditions.

WHAT TO DO IF YOU ACCIDENTALLY SPRAY YOURSELF

In spite of careful precautions, sometimes accidents happen. Here are tips for relief if you accidentally spray yourself with pepper spray:

- Do not touch or rub the affected area. This will spread it and make it worse.

- Remove clothing that has come into contact with pepper spray, and bag it up to keep it separate from other clothes.

- Wash the area with lots of cool water.

- Do not use anything oily or greasy on the area.

- If the discomfort persists, get checked out by a doctor.

HOW LONG DOES PEPPER SPRAY LAST?

Pepper spray comes with an expiration date, usually a year from purchase. The pepper spray itself does not become ineffective over time, but the spraying ability may be compromised. The nozzle may be blocked, or the propellant may no longer work. You don't want to be carrying something to protect yourself and find out that it doesn't work at the time you need it most.

Some manufacturers recommend testing the spray periodically. To do this, go outside and note which way the wind is blowing. Spray away from yourself, making sure the wind is blowing

AWAY from you. However, testing it does cause the product to get used up. To be on the safe side and avoid the risk of accidentally spraying yourself, replace the sprays every 12 to 18 months.

IS IT LEGAL TO CARRY PEPPER SPRAY?

Pepper spray is legal in all 50 states, but some states have certain restrictions in size, strength, and age of carrier (must be over 18 in some states). Check on your own state's regulations or the local police department for rules about carrying pepper spray. It is illegal to carry it anywhere on a plane (whether on your person or in your luggage) and is prohibited in federal and state buildings.

HOW TO USE YOUR PEPPER SPRAY

It should be within easy reach. If you are walking or jogging alone, you should have it either in your hand or front pocket. There is no point having it in your purse or your car's glove box if you are attacked.

Be aware of the nozzle's location and where you are about to spray. If you are outside, be aware of where the wind is blowing. There is a risk of the wind shifting and blowing the spray back to you.

Aim for the attacker's eyes and face.

As soon as your attacker is incapacitated, run away and get help.

Remember, just having pepper spray does not mean you are assured of fending off an attacker. As with many aspects of preparedness, the right mindset will help push the outcome in your favor.

HOMEMADE PEPPER SPRAY

You will need:

2 tablespoons cayenne pepper

¼ cup rubbing alcohol or vodka

1 tablespoon vegetable oil

small plastic container with lid and another similar size container

cheesecloth or small, fine-mesh strainer

funnel

travel-size aerosol spray bottle or recycled eyeglass cleaner spray bottle

Directions:

1. Mix the cayenne pepper and alcohol (or vodka) in the plastic container. Cover tightly and shake. The alcohol will start to change color. Let the mixture sit overnight.

2. Remove the lid and add the vegetable oil. Place the lid back on and shake to mix well. Strain the contents by pouring into the other container using a cheese-cloth or fine-mesh strainer. You are straining the mixture to avoid clogging your spray bottle. Using a funnel, pour the mixture into your aerosol spray bottle.

3. Label the bottle properly and keep out of the reach of children.

ALTERNATIVES TO PEPPER SPRAY

Bear spray contains the same active ingredient as pepper spray, in a much stronger proportion. Bear spray can substitute for pepper spray, but pepper spray cannot substitute for bear spray because it will not have the stopping power needed to incapacitate a bear.

Wasp spray is also widely cited as an alternative to pepper spray, as it can shoot 10 to 20 feet away and is legal in all states. Just be aware that critics of carrying wasp spray for protection always point out that using it for other than the labeled used (i.e., to kill wasps) is technically a violation of federal law (according to the Federal Insecticide, Fungicide, and Rodenticide Act) and may be subject to fines. I would point out that in a life-threatening situation, your safety is the first priority and you will need to use whatever you can to get out of a dangerous situation.

Tasers and Stun Guns

Tasers and stun guns are commonly discussed interchangeably, but they are actually different from each other. They do have a few similarities:

- Both the stun gun and Taser are electronic devices.
- Both are fairly small and can be carried in your pocket or purse.
- Both use some type of battery for power.

- Both are designed to incapacitate the attacker, giving you time to run away and get help.

THE DIFFERENCES

The stun gun requires direct contact between the metal prongs and the attacker. Ideally, a half-second contact will surprise the attacker and cause him to let go, two seconds should impose muscle spasms, and three seconds will cause loss of balance and a dazed mental state. However, I have also found that in some cases, depending on the type of stun gun, you may have to hold contact for up to 4 seconds to get the desired effect. Four seconds is a long time when it comes to an attack. Furthermore, it was found that a person in a drug-induced state or with a high tolerance for pain may be able to resist the effects of the stun gun.

Taser is actually a brand name for a conducted electrical weapon: It works by releasing two fish hook–type prongs toward the attacker, delivering electrical pulses along the wires and into the body. This affects the sensory and motor functions of the person's peripheral nervous system. The general reaction is incapacitation, which could then cause additional injuries when dropping to the ground and/or hitting something. The reaction is not related to pain tolerance since the muscle contractions are involuntary. Also, each Taser probe can penetrate an inch of clothing, including leather.

Law enforcement personnel carry Tasers that have a longer range than commercially available ones.

Price-wise, stun guns cost much less than Tasers, with stun guns priced below $100 and Tasers running in the mid-$300s.

LEGALITY

While legal in 45 states, there are some states that prohibit Tasers and stun guns, such as Hawaii, Massachusetts, New York, New Jersey, Rhode Island, and the District of Columbia. They are legal but with certain restrictions in Connecticut, Illinois, and Wisconsin. Before considering the purchase of either a stun gun or a Taser, always check the laws in your state.

IMPROVISED WEAPONS

If you are attacked and find yourself without a weapon, you may need to reach for common items found around your vicinity that can be used against your attacker. If you use these items properly, you can at least incapacitate or delay whoever is threatening you, allowing you time to escape and call the authorities for help.

- office supplies: pen, stapler, letter opener, paper weight, scissors
- kitchen utensils: knives, cast iron pan, ice pick, hot coffee, boiling water
- tools: hammer, nail gun, heavy wrench, tire iron, garden tools such as hoe, shovel, or rake
- sports equipment: baseball bat, tennis racquet, golf clubs, dumbbells

- chemicals: hairspray, bleach, anti-freeze, fire extinguisher, bug spray
- loose change (Place this in a sock or sturdy bag to hit an attacker in the face or other vulnerable area.)
- heavy flashlight, such as the Mag Lite
- rocks

LAYERING WEAPONS

Some self-defense experts "layer" their defense plans by having various self-defense methods at their disposal: pepper spray spread out in inconspicuous areas around the house (must not be within reach of kids), stun gun or Taser on their person, and finally, a firearm. They prefer to have various options before having to resort to lethal force.

FIREARMS

A discussion about defending yourself would not be complete without including firearms. Unfortunately, there are certain elements of society who would not hesitate to resort to violence or murder to take what they want from others regardless of the consequences. In a disaster or down-grid situation where no help is available, these ruthless elements may become even more aggressive or desperate. Fortunately, the Second Amendment assures all Americans the right to keep and bear arms. I recommend you take the steps to legally own a firearm and learn how to use it.

That said, the decision to purchase a firearm is a highly personal choice. Consider all the ramifications before you go out and make a purchase: Would you be able to fire on another human being and under what circumstances would you be able to do so? What are your state's laws regarding the owning of firearms? Do you have young children whom you need to protect as well as keep away from firearms? How does your partner feel about it? You must also be willing to commit to fully learning how to safely operate a firearm.

At minimum, many preppers own a handgun, a shotgun, and a rifle for self-defense. These weapons may also be used for hunting purposes.

Handguns

The first handgun I ever used for target shooting was a revolver. I found it much easier to use than a semiautomatic. It is simple to load and easy to maintain and operate. The downside is revolvers only have six shots, while semiautomatic handguns have nine or more. As I gained more confidence and got more training, I started practicing with a semiautomatic.

HOW TO CHOOSE A HANDGUN WISELY

First and foremost, a handgun must fit the size of your hands, allowing you to have a proper grip so you will feel comfortable shooting with it. For maximum control, grip the handgun with two hands: If you are right-handed, clasp your left hand over your right hand's fingers. Be careful where you place your left hand, particularly the thumb.

Popular pistols are .9 mm, .40 caliber, and .45 caliber. Choosing the caliber is based on your own personal needs. Handgun prices vary from $300 and up, so choose wisely.

As mentioned above, if you are new to guns, take a basic shooting class that emphasizes safety.

Shotguns

Many security experts consider shotguns to be ideal for home protection. They work well at close range and do not need a lot of accuracy as long as you aim in the general direction of your target. Choices are the 12 gauge or the 20 gauge, which is slightly smaller.

I have tried both and found the 12 gauge to be heavy, with a powerful kick. For a smaller-framed person, the 20 gauge is a lot lighter and has less of a kick than the 12 gauge.

The ammunition for shotguns or shotgun shells are fairly inexpensive and readily available at most sporting goods stores.

Some shotguns make quite the recoil; you could potentially get a bruise on your hand or shoulder if it takes you by surprise. Take the time to practice loading and firing your shotgun; go to a gun range that allows shotgun usage.

Rifles

Rifles are recommended for hunting and shooting long distance. A good starter rifle for beginners is the .22 rifle—it is lightweight and easy to shoot. It would not be useful for hunting deer and other large game, but will suffice for rabbits and other small animals. The ammunition for this rifle is also inexpensive, making it a good rifle to use for target practice.

Gun safety and training courses are offered at shooting ranges, sporting goods stores, gun stores, and even community colleges at reasonable prices. Project Appleseed is offered by a nonprofit organization, the Revolutionary War Veterans Association. Their goal is to share information about the Founding Fathers, history, and civics and to teach rifle marksmanship skills. They have a 2-day program, usually done on weekends, that teaches traditional rifle marksmanship from standing, sitting/ kneeling, and prone positions. As of this writing, the cost for 2 days is $60 for adults and $20 for children under 18. For more information, visit AppleSeedInfo.org.

The National Rifle Association also offers firearm training instruction in various cities throughout the year at reasonable prices. Their beginner courses include basic pistol, rifle, or shotgun training, personal protection inside or outside the home, marksman training, safety courses, etc. For more information, visit NRAInstructors.org.

RULES OF GUN SAFETY

- Treat every gun as though it were loaded. Anytime you pick up a firearm, assume it is loaded. Check to make sure there is no bullet lodged in the magazine and chamber.

- Always keep the gun pointed in a safe direction.

- Always be sure of what you are shooting at and what else is beyond your target. Never point at anything you do not intend to shoot.

- Keep your finger away from the trigger until you are ready to shoot.

- Know how to use your gun.

- Use the correct ammunition.

- Be sure the barrel is clear of obstructions before shooting.

- Never use alcohol or drugs if you will be handling a firearm.

- Guns and ammunition should be stored separately in a locked area, inaccessible to kids.

- Do not shoot at hard surfaces or water as the bullet may ricochet.

- Do not engage in horseplay with a loaded firearm. Though it is strictly a personal choice and handled according to your beliefs, consider what type of training you will give your children regarding proper gun safety and handling.

Where to Buy Your First Gun

You can either buy guns in person or online.

Online: Gun dealers and auctioneers sell guns online. Unless you are an experienced gun owner and purchaser, it is advisable to buy a gun in person. Buying online, you can only view photos. You will not be able to closely inspect and hold the weapon as you would in person. Buying online from an out-of-state dealer has certain requirements. You would be required to have the purchased gun shipped to a Federal Firearms Licensed (FFL) dealer in your state. The FFL dealer handles all the legal paperwork involved with transferring the gun to your name. Typically, the FFL dealer charges around $50 or thereabouts per transaction, which adds to your overall cost.

In person: You can purchase firearms from gun stores, sporting goods stores, gun ranges, pawn shops, estate sales, and gun shows.

Gun shows are held in many cities several times during the year. They are usually held on weekends, and many gun buyers feel they can get good prices at gun shows. Keep these tips in mind when visiting a gun show:

Guns are not the only things you can purchase. There is a large variety of items that can be found, such as ammunition, knives, water purifiers, lighters/fire starters, freeze-dried food, beef jerky, concealed carry purses, T-shirts, books, etc. Concession stands carry snacks and drinks but can be on the expensive side, so bring snacks and bottled water to avoid paying premium prices.

Do your research beforehand and know what you want to buy. This advice applies wherever you decide to buy your firearm. Knowledgeable sales people are always happy to answer questions, but having an idea what you want to buy and how prices compare elsewhere is definitely an advantage for the buyer.

Many vendors offer a cash discount.

If you decide to make an impulse purchase while at the gun show, you can at least compare prices among various sellers. I have seen a $20 to $80 difference in pricing among gun show sellers.

A good strategy is to peruse all the sellers in the show from one end to the other, look at everything, and narrow down your choices among three to four vendors.

Larger shows have more vendors and therefore a better selection, as there is competition among sellers.

Frequently, dealers have prices that are discounted for "show only" purposes. Once the discounted items are sold, they are gone, so it is best to come early.

Some vendors are open to haggling, but some are not. Or, they may be willing to throw in certain items as a bonus. It never hurts to ask.

Chapter 10

WHEN YOU'RE ON THE MOVE

Disaster can strike at any time. We all hope to be at home when it happens, since that is where most of our supplies are located, but there is no guarantee. Very few people stay at home all day. Most of us have to go to work, take our kids to school, go shopping, attend church, and go about many other commitments that take us away from home. Commuting to work alone may take from a few minutes to an hour or more, depending on where you live.

In an emergency, the only useful supplies are the ones you happen to have with you. Rather than having just one emergency kit stored at home, it is preferable to "layer your preps," or have several layers of emergency backup items spread out among various areas: the office, your vehicle, your person ("everyday carry" or EDC), and of course, at home.

To avoid becoming overwhelmed with expenses, collect these items gradually. Budget for one area each month, according to what you can afford.

YOUR EVERYDAY CARRY (EDC) GEAR

Preppers get into a lot discussions about what goes into their EDC gear. These are items you would rely on, often on a daily basis, to get you out of a bind or even just to make things more convenient for yourself. There really is no right answer as to what should go into your EDC: It all depends on your daily activities. But there are a few common denominators. EDC gear should be:

- small and portable
- easy to carry
- filled with things you depend on daily
- filled with emergency items you'd hopefully never use but that are great when you need them, such as defensive items, a firestarter, etc.

Your everyday carry gear is always subject to change according to your activities. Here are some examples of common everyday carry gear:

- cell phone
- firestarter or book of matches
- key ring items: flashlight, Swiss Army knife
- paracord bracelet

- pen
- pepper spray, taser or stun gun, or pistol (only if you have a license to carry a concealed weapon)
- mini first aid kit (page 124)
- solar watch
- sunglasses
- wallet that includes ID, insurance information, debit card, and $20 cash

PARACORD

Paracord is a lightweight nylon cord that was originally used for parachutes in World War II. Also known as 550 cord, paracord has multiple uses for everyday life as well as emergencies. It's made of interwoven nylon strands that are fairly elastic. You can use the inner strands as a substitute for dental floss, sewing thread, fishing line, or to suture a wound. Paracord can be used as a clothesline, to secure gear to the top of your car, as a replacement for shoelaces, to make an arm sling, as a tow rope, as a leash, as a belt to hold up your pants, to hold up a tarp for shelter, etc. In an emergency, you can unwind your paracord bracelet for its multiple uses.

OFFICE EMERGENCIES

A few years ago, while working at a highrise downtown, I was in an elevator full of people when it suddenly stopped. The lights flickered and turned off for a few seconds before turning back on. The elevator stayed still for several minutes: At first, people looked at each other uncomfortably and made a few awkward jokes. Someone hit the emergency alarm to alert building security about our stalled elevator. Thankfully, the elevator started moving shortly after and everyone breathed a sigh of relief. Our building had a power outage and the emergency backup system took a few minutes to activate. When we got to our floors, everything was dimly lit. All but one elevator was working and there was a huge crowd waiting for it. I did not want to get stuck in the building so I grabbed my laptop, took the stairs to the parking garage, and left.

The experience showed me the need for an emergency kit at my desk at work. Here are the items to include in an office emergency kit. Most of these items are inexpensive and easy to collect:

- 1 (12-pack) of bottled water
- comfortable shoes
- compass
- deodorant
- emergency weather radio with extra batteries
- extra jacket
- feminine hygiene items
- flashlight with extra batteries
- hand-sanitizing wipes
- light sticks
- mini sewing kit
- multitool
- Mylar blankets

- nonperishable foods, such as canned tuna, crackers, canned, and dried fruits
- pry bar
- safety pins
- small first aid kit
- toothbrush, mini toothpaste, floss
- umbrella

Prepping items you can find at the dollar store include bottled water, mini sewing kit, safety pins, Mylar blankets, hand sanitizing wipes, lightsticks, mini toothbrushes, and floss. I prefer to buy first aid supplies, batteries, flashlights, and other gear at discount or department stores.

My office emergency kit has helped me in several ways, and is not just for disasters. It has been very handy on days I'd forgotten to bring lunch, felt ill at work, or experienced unexpected weather changes.

In a study involving World Trade Center 9/11 evacuees, a large number of respondents indicated they were unfamiliar with the safety features, evacuation routes, and building plans of their workplace. This is still very common today: Most office workers, unless they are part of the emergency team, do not know where all emergency exits are located. To avoid getting trapped in your office building:

- Take the time to find out where all the floor and building exits are located. Plan a route on how you would get out of your floor. Visit your building's management office and view a map of the premises if you have to.

- Know your own office's emergency plan.

- Learn all the exits out of your parking garage.

- Map several routes out of the city; know which route to take in case you have to walk.

- Keep your cell phone charged at all times.

- Don't panic.

- Ladies: Avoid foot injuries in case of debris by immediately changing out of your high-heels into comfortable walking shoes.

- Don't waste time: Once you have decided to evacuate, don't try to finish up work, clean your desk, or mill around the office.

- Don't ignore your intuition. If your gut tells you it's time to leave, you should safely do so.

"GET HOME BAG" AKA CAR EMERGENCY KIT

In a previous job, I drove 50 miles to work each way, which translated to about a 1½-hour commute in the morning and evening. Some coworkers had an even longer commute. We spend so much time in our cars, it only makes sense to keep emergency supplies handy there at all times.

Although many may consider it a separate thing, I count on the car emergency kit to double as your "Get Home Bag," supplies that will help you find your way home in an emergency. If you are away from home when an emergency happens, you more than likely traveled via your car and therefore would need your car and the supplies therein to get you home.

Before buying anything, check to make sure the owner's manual, spare tire, and jack are in your car. Most people assume these items come with the car and don't check on them until they really need them. Don't take anything for granted: Look for them now. If they are not in the car, check around your garage and find them.

To assemble a basic car care kit, include roadside flares, reflective tape, safety triangles, jumper cables, a flashlight with extra batteries, light sticks, and Fix-a-Flat (or another type of sealant for the tires). Because Fix-a-Flat is a one-use item, replace it as soon as you use it. Here are other essentials for your car emergency kit.

First aid kit. As mentioned earlier in this section, layering your preparedness systems by having supplies in key places makes a lot of sense. You may already have an office first aid kit, but that won't do you any good if you come across an emergency on the road.

Buy a preassembled first aid kit or build one yourself. Make sure you include pain relievers, allergy medicine, antacids, adhesive tape, antibacterial wipes, antiseptic cream, and other medications your family uses.

Food. Keep 3 days' worth of portable, filling, and non-perishable foods such as granola bars, protein bars, or high-calorie food bars. After 3 months, eat and replace. Cars get very hot in the summer, which will affect most foods. They may not spoil right away, but taste and quality will deteriorate.

Water. Bring enough bottled water for the family to last for 3 days. Eight- to twelve-ounce water bottles are fairly inexpensive. Buy them on sale or as loss leaders for maximum savings. You should use them up and replace them before the year is up to avoid waste.

Weather-appropriate supplies. For cold weather, include Mylar blankets, hand warmers, gloves and weather-appropriate clothing, windshield ice scraper, snow shovel, tire chains, and rock salt or cat litter for tire traction. For warm weather, include sunscreen or sunblock, and bug spray. An umbrella and rain ponchos are useful additions in the case of rain.

Other helpful items:

- cash in assorted denominations, including change for toll roads
- compass
- duct tape
- fire extinguisher
- lighters
- matches
- multitool or Swiss Army knife
- paper maps (*Tip:* Maps may be obtained for free from roadside assistance clubs.)
- paracord
- portable stove
- radio (battery-operated or hand-crank)

- rags
- seat belt cutter/window breaker escape tool
- tow strap or tow rope
- trash bags

If you have kids: Pack extra clothes, socks, diapers, baby wipes, small toys, and books.

For pet owners: Bring your pet carrier, collar, leash, extra pet food, and water bowls.

What about toilet emergencies while in the car? For liquid waste, you can use a product called TravelJohn Disposable Urinal Bags. When used, the material turns into an odorless gel substance. There are also portable urinals available, with adapters for women. A wide-mouth bottle could suffice as well. For solid waste, you can use a 5-gallon portable toilet (see page 135 for DIY instructions).

Don't take any chances—get that car survival kit assembled now. Hopefully, you'll never need it, but if you ever get stuck, you'll be glad you do.

BUGGING OUT

Bugging out means leaving your home due to a natural or man-made disaster. The question of whether to shelter in place (stay put) or leave your home (bug out) is possibly the most hotly debated topics in the preparedness world. There are a lot of advantages to staying in your home: You have all your supplies with you, you know the area, and you do not have to travel and fight unknown dangers. On the other hand, you may be forced to bug out even if you don't want to. The natural or man-made disaster may have made your area unsuitable for living; evacuation may be imminent due to fire, hurricane, or tsunami warning; the infrastructure may be damaged; a pandemic could be nearby; or lawlessness due to the absence of law enforcement may put you at risk.

Where Would You Go?

You will need to give yourself a few options in regards to choosing a destination in the event that you had to leave your home. For example, if there were a hurricane heading your way, you might contact some relatives in another city within your state who are not in the path of the hurricane and ask to stay with them for a few days. Or, you may find a hotel or motel that is far enough away and stay there for a few days until the hurricane has passed. Finally, if none of these choices is available, you may just visit another family at another state all together and spend a few days with them.

I recommend having at least three choices: A, B, and C destinations. That way, if one option does not work, you have others to try out.

The same thing would apply if you had to leave your home permanently: Have at least three destinations in mind.

What to Include in a Bug Out Bag

You will need a container for all your bug out supplies. Any container large enough to fit your supplies and gear is good enough when you are starting out. When I first started assembling my bug out supplies, I used a large plastic bin with a lid, similar to Rubbermaid bins used to store Christmas decorations. You would simply load the whole bin in the car and bug out. The downside to this type of container is that it is not portable if you had to travel on foot.

Later, I decided it was time for a backpack. My first purchase was a military-style backpack that got good reviews from survivalist sites. It didn't turn out well for me. When I received it and tried carrying gear with it, I found it was much too large and heavy for my frame. An ill-fitting backpack can cause back and shoulder strain. Avoid wasting money by visiting a brick-and-mortar store and trying on several backpacks before buying. Note the style and model number and compare prices before actually making the purchase.

The backpack should be lightweight but roomy and sturdy. It should fit your frame well. The weight should rest on your hips instead of your shoulders. You'll also want a pack that looks plain and nondescript as opposed to one that screams "Look at me, I have tons of gear!"

You can find good, reasonably priced backpacks at sports and outdoor stores, such as REI, Academy, Gander Mountain, etc. Sign up for their mailing lists and wait for sales. Adjust the backpack to your size; a salesperson can add weights to it so you can walk around and try it on for comfort. Having the added weights will show you where it can chafe or pull so you can adjust the straps accordingly.

Pack carefully: The backpack should weigh no more than 30 percent of your weight.

The bug out bag is also known as the 72-hour kit, as its contents should sustain you for 72 hours. Don't forget to bring cash and some entertainment items to keep the kids happy, such as books and playing cards. Now we can go over the basic areas you need to cover:

MEDICINES:

- allergy medicine (Benadryl, Zyrtec, Allegra, or Claritin)
- antidiarrheal medicine (Imodium)
- anti-nausea medicine (Dramamine)
- pain relievers such as acetaminophen (Tylenol), aspirin (Bayer), and ibuprofen (Advil or Motrin)
- any personal prescription medicines, such as blood pressure pills, asthma inhalers, birth control pills, etc.

Note: If you have children, you will need children's medications as well.

WOUND AND SKIN CARE:

- Ace bandages
- alcohol wipes
- aloe vera for sunburns
- antibiotic ointment (Neosporin)
- antiseptic wipes
- assorted adhesive bandages
- burn cream
- sterile gauze pads and medical tape

EYE CARE:

- extra pairs of glasses, contact lenses, and contact lens solution
- eye drops (Visine)
- eye wash cup

HYGIENE SUPPLIES:

- detergent (page 157)
- hand sanitizer
- insect repellent
- sanitary napkins or tampons*
- shampoo
- soap
- sunscreen or sunblock
- toilet paper (remove cardboard insert and flatten)
- toothbrush, toothpaste

* Quick tip: Individually wrapped tampons and sanitary napkins may also be used as improvised wound dressing as they are very absorbent.

WASTE DISPOSAL:

- folding shovel
- heavy-duty garbage bags

MISCELLANEOUS:

- magnifying glass
- multivitamins
- oral thermometer
- sterile gloves
- tweezers

Food: Bring lightweight, easy-to-prepare food, such as high-calorie energy bars, jerky, instant oatmeal, crackers, freeze-dried foods, and MREs (page 86). Canned foods are good too, if you can accommodate the weight, but you will need a can opener. Take a few candy bars for quick energy and a morale boost. Take a few packets of instant coffee or tea for your morning beverage.

Water: Because water is critical for survival, you'll need to carry enough to last you until you find your next water source. Store at least 3 liters in your 72-hour kit. Some good containers include collapsible water bladders, BPA-free water bottles, etc. You'll need a way to purify water, so you should have a portable water filter, bleach, and iodine water purification tablets. Pack a few coffee filters as well, so you can eliminate soil and solids from the water before running it through the filter. This will lengthen the life of your water filter.

Utensils: Pack a lightweight mess kit with a metal pot, kettle, plate, cup, and spork. A lightweight backpacking stove with a fuel canister should be sufficient for cooking food.

Fire: Fire is essential to survival as it provides warmth, comfort, light, a way to cook food or signal your location, and a measure of protection against bugs and predators. You would need several means to make a fire, such as matches, lighters, and a magnesium fire starter. Experts also recommend bringing instant tinder, such as Insta-Fire or WetFire. However, if you are on a budget, here are some ideas to make your own:

- Take 10 to 20 cotton balls and slather them with petroleum jelly. Store in an empty pill container, mint tin, or zip-top bag.

- Here's an even cheaper option: Remove dryer lint from the lint trap of your clothes dryer. With a handful of lint, scoop up petroleum jelly and saturate the dryer lint. Separate the lint into small, nickel-sized pieces. Store in a waterproof container.

- You can even use potato chips or Fritos corn chips as tinder.

- Make your own char cloth.

CHAR CLOTH

Char cloth is a highly combustible material that is portable, lightweight, and easy to make. Having char cloth will increase your chances of success when trying to ignite a fire with a spark. It can be made with items you likely already have at home:

You will need:

100 percent cotton cloth (use old T-shirts, jeans, etc.)

small tin that can seal shut, such as an Altoids tin or other mint tin

scissors

nail or small screwdriver so you can poke holes in the tin

tongs

oven mitt

pill bottle

Directions:

1. Cut the cloth into small pieces that will fit in the mint tin (approximately 2 x 2 inches). Lay them flat on the mint tin and close it.

2. Poke a very small hole on top of the tin using the nail or small screwdriver.

3. Place the sealed container in a small fire, such as a fireplace or barbecue grill.

4. You will see smoke coming out of the hole in the can. When the smoke stops coming out, turn the can over using the tongs. Allow the same amount of time as the previous side.

5. Using the tongs, remove the tin from the fire and lay it on heat-resistant surface. Use an oven mitt to open the can. The cloth should appear blackened, with stiffened texture.

6. Store the cooled pieces of char cloth in an old pill bottle and store in your bug out bag.

7. To make a fire using the char cloth, lay it on some natural tinder, such as bark shavings, dried grass, or leaves and send the spark directly on the char cloth. It should ignite. Blow on it enough for the fire to spread throughout the natural tinder. Place with the rest of the firewood and now you have the fire going.

Clothing: Dress in weather-appropriate clothing. If possible, dress in layers. Pack 3 days' worth of clothes, including underwear and socks. Wool socks are the best for wicking moisture away from your feet. For maximum comfort, wear sock liners under your wool socks to avoid blisters. For sun protection, wear sunglasses, a hat, and a bandanna. I'd also recommend bringing some instant hand warmers and work gloves to protect your hands from injury when hauling branches, gathering firewood, or even sifting through debris.

Footwear: A pair of comfortable hiking boots would be the best choice for bugging out. You may be walking along rough terrain or debris-strewn paths and need shoes that will protect your feet. Choose ankle-high, lightweight boots that are also sturdy. They should be water-resistant and have non-slip soles. Make sure you break in your shoes as soon as you buy them. Bugging out in a disaster should not be the first time you are using your boots.

BREAKING IN YOUR BOOTS

Wear them around the house for a day or two. Next, start wearing the shoes on short hikes. If you feel a blister coming on, remove your shoes as soon as possible and place a Band-Aid or moleskin pad on the blister. Do not wait until you are in pain, as the blister will only get worse. Continue to wear your boots until they are completely comfortable. Store them close to you in case of sudden emergency.

Shelter: Pack a lightweight tent as your bug out shelter. The size would depend on your family size. It should be a three-season tent, unless you live in an extremely frigid area. Choose a tent with aluminum stakes instead of steel. You will want a ground tarp and a rain fly for your tent to keep moisture out.

For extra warmth, pack a small wool blanket as well as Mylar emergency blankets.

You will also need a lightweight sleeping bag that is appropriate for your environment. Sleeping bags come with a degree rating, which is the lowest temperature at which the sleeping bag can be used comfortably. For example, a sleeping bag that is rated at 20 degrees means it will be comfortable when the temperature is at 20 degrees. For most areas and for budget purposes, a rating of 30 degrees will suffice. I like the mummy-style sleeping bag as it comes with a hood that will trap heat, keeping you warmer even as the temperature dips below the degree rating. Pack your sleeping bag in a compression sack to reduce the size.

Lighting: Don't get caught in the dark! Pack a few lighting options, such as flashlights and camping headlamps, along with extra batteries for each.

Tools:

- ax
- binoculars
- carabiner
- duct tape
- fishing kit
- knife, knife sharpener
- mirror for signaling
- multitool
- paper maps and compass
- paracord
- rope
- safety pins
- saw
- sewing kit

Communications: Wear a whistle and pack a small mirror to use for signaling your location. If you are traveling with a group, two-way radios are extremely helpful for reaching others in the group. Keep your cell phone fully charged and bring a solar charger for backup power. There is a chance that cell phones may not work; however, texting may still work. Keep track of emergency alerts with an AM/FM/NOAA Weather radio, preferably with solar or hand-crank backup power options. Don't forget to pack spare batteries.

Weapons: Unfortunately, criminal types do not stop operating during emergencies; if anything, they'll take advantage of the situation as law enforcement will be occupied dealing with disaster calls. You will need a way to protect yourself. At the minimum, bring pepper spray or bear spray. A stun gun, Taser, and firearm with ammunition are other options. Always be mindful of the laws in your state regarding carrying these weapons.

Documents: You'll need to take important documents with you, such as passports, birth certificates, social security cards, driver's licenses or state identification, proof of home or auto ownership, health, life, home, and auto insurance papers, concealed carry license, etc. Bring your grab-and-go binder (page 230) with your printed emergency contact list. Other important documents, such as medical information, vaccination records, wills, etc., can be scanned and stored in a flash drive.

Your Bug-Out Vehicle

In the event of an evacuation, you will be relying on your vehicle to get you out of danger.

At one time, our family only had one fuel-efficient compact car that was excellent for driving around the city. After one season of heavy rains and flooding, we realized the need for a larger, more rugged vehicle that would not get damaged the next time a heavy downpour caused high water in the streets. After seeing so many smaller cars stall out and get stranded in our city's flooded streets, we decided to buy a used SUV.

Most people already own a vehicle and may not be able to afford a specific "bug out vehicle." You can evaluate what you own right now and consider the following:

- Number of people who will be riding with you
- Trunk/storage space
- Gas mileage
- Ability to drive in flooding and rough terrain
- Condition of the car

If you feel you do not have a lot of room in your car, you can take some steps now to increase your storage space by investigating these options: adding a roof rack or rooftop cargo bag, or attaching a cargo carrier behind your vehicle.

Keep your vehicle well-maintained and keep your fuel tank at least half full at all times in case of emergency. If you know you will be driving long distances, carry 5 to 10 gallons of gasoline in a spill-proof gasoline safety can.

Tips to Save Money on Gear

Right about now you may be wondering how you are ever going to afford all this gear. The good news is, you don't have to get everything all at once. Even if you focus on covering just one item a month, you are still on your way to being prepared.

Your tent and sleeping bags are likely to be the most expensive items in your bug out bag. They also last for several years. Try to buy the best quality you can afford to, but shop wisely. Start by looking at good brands that work for your budget, but do not buy at the first place that you find them. Compare prices among various stores, and also check out eBay or Craigslist for quality, used items.

If you are bugging out with your family, you do not need to duplicate the gear for each family member, except for personal items such as clothing, shoes, etc. Also, if you know a like-minded group who is also focused on preparedness, you can buy some items in bulk and split the cost amongst you.

Take up camping or backpacking as a hobby and you will get a lot of use out of the gear, as they double as recreational items. You'll also get to practice outdoor skills, as covered in the next chapter.

Chapter 11

LOW-COST SURVIVAL AND PREPAREDNESS PROJECTS

Throughout this book, I have discussed survival needs and steps to address those needs in a disaster. But there is one aspect you need to conquer on your own: your mind. You can have the greatest gear in the world and own a fully stocked rural retreat, but to be truly prepared, you must adopt a prepared mindset.

RECOGNIZE "NORMALCY BIAS"

Normalcy bias is a mental state that causes a person to be in denial: They assume that something terrible that never happened before surely can never happen to them. Because of the inability to face the reality of a disaster, the person with normalcy bias is unable to prepare for a disaster before it happens. It is a coping mechanism that can have dire results. Much like an ostrich that buries its head in the sand, a person experiencing it refuses to see what's happening right before their eyes. Even when the emergency does happen, the person is unable cope and respond properly.

When Hurricane Katrina hit New Orleans, there were many warnings about its unprecedented size and power; however, many residents and even city officials did not make appropriate plans to prepare or evacuate. This paralyzed them from taking appropriate actions. In order to recognize how normalcy bias can hamper you, do some mental exercises by imagining certain situations and how you would react to them. It does not have to be anything difficult or mentally exhausting. Whenever I watch disaster movies, such as *The Day After Tomorrow*, *Independence Day*, or even outrageous zombie flicks, I imagine myself in the characters' shoes and how I might react if I were placed in such a precarious situation. What would you if you were placed in the following scenarios? Ask yourself, "What would I do if..."

- I were walking to my car and I noticed someone were following me.
- There was shooting in the mall where I happened to be shopping.
- A thief broke into my house while I was at home.
- A tornado (wildfire, or your most likely peril) is threatening my home.

MAKE A PLAN

Always be mindful of what's going on around you and what can potentially happen at any time. So many people go about their days on autopilot, constantly playing with their phones or tablets and not aware of their surroundings. We multitask in our heads, thinking about what we need to do and living several hours into the future. I am guilty of this and constantly have to pull myself back into the present moment.

Consider what you would do if a disaster were to happen while you and your spouse were at work and the kids at school. Who will pick up the kids? Where can you pick them up if the school is forced to shut down? Every school has a record of backup emergency contacts. If you designate other family members to pick up your kids in the event you are unable to do so, make sure the school has a record of it. Otherwise, the school may not release them.

Know the emergency policy in your workplace as well as in the schools. When is a lockdown instituted? Which exits will be closed in an emergency? All these questions must be answered well ahead of an actual emergency. It doesn't cost you anything to start finding out this information, so you can make plans to prepare. Designate an alternate meeting place in the event your home becomes unsafe or inaccessible.

If power is out, electric door openers in security buildings and gated communities may not work. This actually happened to me during a power outage. I was living in a secure apartment community that had electric gates leading to my unit's garage. I had locked the front door with a deadbolt from the inside so the front door was out of the question. The only way in was through the garage. Building maintenance was unable to open the gate manually. I had to sit in the car for hours waiting for the power to come back. Have a backup plan on what you would do should this happen.

Even if you don't live in a gated area, accidents, floods, trees blocking exits can happen. Become familiar with all the possible ways in and out of your neighborhood.

Map out various routes home as well as out of the city. Navigate your alternate routes to avoid getting stuck in a never-ending traffic nightmare. A few years ago, Houston residents all tried to leave at the same time right before an impending Hurricane Rita. The freeways became clogged with traffic, with people running out of gas in the middle of the freeway. Friends who experienced this nightmare can remember a normal 2-hour drive stretching to 8 hours. Some people left their cars in the gridlocked traffic to search for a bathroom by a nearby exit or to find food. Upon returning to their cars an hour or two later, they found the traffic had not even moved. If you plan to evacuate, you need to be among the first; take an underused alternate route or you may be stuck in gridlock.

Build a calling or texting tree (page 165).

Create a grab-and-go binder. What is a grab-and-go binder? It is a storage binder containing all your important documents that you can easily grab while heading out in an emergency. Collect all your important documents such as:

- birth certificates
- deed to your house
- lease agreement
- mortgage documents
- car ownership or "pink slip"
- photos of your driver's license
- immunization records
- home or renter's insurance
- auto and life insurance policies
- passports
- school records
- social security card

Include any records that you feel may be needed in case you need to start over somewhere else. Keep this binder safe as it contains a lot of personal information that are sought after by identity thieves.

Back up your photos and recipes. During the 2015 flooding disaster in Houston, many families were dismayed to see old family photos soaked in the floodwaters and sought restoration services to salvage them. Similarly, old family recipes are highly valued and would be sorely missed should they be lost in a disaster. Find ways to protect these items before an emergency happens. Create electronic backups of your favorite photos and recipes, and save them in a thumb drive.

Also consider saving them online. Several cloud-based storage provider, currently offer free storage. As of this writing, Dropbox, iCloud Drive, Microsoft OneDrive, and Google Drive offer free storage up to a certain limit. They start charging a monthly fee if you want to upgrade to more than the allotted free space.

Take a weekend to print out your contact list from your cell phone into a hard copy or address book. Better yet, memorize some of the important phone numbers and stop relying on your cell phone for everything.

If you lost access to your cell phone, would you be able to contact your loved ones? So many of us rely on our smart phones to reach anyone, but in an emergency, cell reception may be interrupted. Even on a normal day, your cell phone can run out of power and until you can charge it, you cannot turn it back on. Years ago, I was speaking with my daughter and my phone's charge ran out. I did not have my phone charger with me. I wanted to call my daughter back on a landline but realized her number was stored in the cell phone, which would not even turn on. I had to wait until I got home to charge the phone and call my daughter. I resolved to memorize all of my frequently called phone numbers. I also stored these numbers in an address book.

Try being "off the grid" for a weekend and see how well you do. We have all become overly reliant on technology. It may be an eye-opening experience. The parameters are all up to you and the family would have to be involved.

- Can you find your way without GPS, using a paper map alone?
- Can you turn off your phone and unhook yourself from texting and social media?
- What would you do for entertainment?
- Can you cook food without electricity?

Identify water sources near your home. If water were to become scarce, do you have natural water sources near your home? Identify locations of streams, rivers, or lakes as potential water sources. Map out a route to these water sources in case you have to utilize them in an emergency.

Test your equipment. This is one step that many preppers often neglect. I hear a lot of comments about people buying the necessary gear for emergencies but immediately storing them away in the closet for when the disaster happens. Taking the first step of buying gear is great, but the equipment needs to be tested. Opening the box and reading the instructions for the first time should not happen just as the disaster unfolds. Learn how to use your equipment, such as a water purifier, backup stove, and solar chargers well before an emergency happens. Practice setting up your tent; try setting it up in the dark. People experience a tremendous amount of stress during disasters, and learning to use gear for the first time or finding out you got the wrong batteries or the wrong fuel will just add to the tense situation.

Conduct a fire drill. You will need to get your whole family involved before holding the fire drill. Discuss what everyone should do in case of fire.

- Walk through the entire house: Know where all the smoke detectors are located and test them; identify all your exits and the location of the fire extinguisher. If you have bars on your windows, make sure the escape latches work. Show everyone how to stay low to the ground to avoid smoke inhalation. Show older children how to use a fire extinguisher. Decide on a safe meeting place outside the house. Call 911 when out of the house. Once outside, there is no going back inside the burning building.

- Once everyone is familiar with what needs to be done in case of fire, you can conduct the fire drill. It can be either night or day, as long as everyone is at home. Use a whistle or alarm to announce the "fire." Get everyone evacuated as quickly as possible as though you were in a real fire. Try to get everyone out within 3 minutes. Discuss how your drill went—what went well, what did not go so smoothly, and how it can be improved.

Learn how to shut off your home's utilities. In the aftermath of a disaster, you may have to turn off your water main, gas, or electricity. Most shut-off valves are tucked away in unobtrusive places, so you may have to do a bit of searching around before you find them. Don't wait until a disaster to learn where your shut off valves are location.

Gas: In an emergency, you may have to turn off the gas if you smell gas or hear a hissing sound, signs that indicate a possible gas leak. Get everyone out of the house for safety. If you do turn off the gas, you must never turn it back on yourself; this requires a gas company technician or a licensed plumber.

- The gas shut-off valve is likely to be located next to the gas meter, usually outside your home, in the back of the house or on the side. Facing the meter, you will see a pipe that goes from the ground to the meter. The shut off valve is on that pipe, approximately 6 inches or so above the ground. You can tell the gas is on if the valve is parallel to the gas pipe. To shut off the gas, use a crescent wrench and turn the valve 90 degrees. Note, you can also use a water and gas shut-off tool, also known as a "4 in 1 tool," which costs between $15 and $20.

- If you are unable to locate the gas shut-off valve, call your gas company and find out where it is before an emergency happens.

Water: If a water pipe suddenly leaks, you will need to shut off the water as soon as possible to avoid flooding and expensive repairs. For homes in warm areas, the water shut-off valve is likely next to an exterior wall or in an underground box with a lid. In colder climates, where there is more likelihood of freezing, the shut-off valve would likely be inside the house, in the basement or some other warm area.

Electricity: Turn off power only in an extreme emergency, such as a flood in your home or a gas leak. Turn off all running appliances and unplug laptops before turning off power. It is a good idea to take a flashlight with you if you plan on turning off the power in your entire house.

- The circuit breaker or fuse box is usually a metal box located inside your home.
- DO NOT touch the electrical panel if it is wet, if the floor you are stepping on is wet, or if you see exposed wires.

- The panel will have the main power switch on top, and individual breakers for different parts of the house. To turn off power to an individual breaker, flip the switch to "off." To turn off power to the whole house, flip the main breaker switch to "off." The flashlight will come in handy at this point, since the entire house will go dark.

Get to know your neighbors. These days, you can live in the same neighborhood for years and never know your neighbors. However, in a disaster, neighborhoods may have to band together for safety or assistance. Even if an emergency never happens in your area, it is a good idea to get to know the families around you, if only to keep an eye out for each other. Chat with your neighbor when you see them across the fence, or organize a block party or neighborhood garage sale. You may find like-minded people and maybe make a friend or two. If you have a group of preparedness-minded folks, you can also share equipment or split bulk purchases.

Learn survivalist skills. Knowing how to survive in the wild without the aid of gear and technology will allow you to survive anywhere. Gaining knowledge weighs and costs nothing, giving any penny-pinching prepper the ultimate advantage.

As you pick up on the survival skills outlined below, consider getting into shape. Day-to-day survival can be very strenuous for the average person who is not used to looking for water sources, building shelter, or gathering firewood.

HOW TO START A FIRE FOR SURVIVAL

Learn at least three alternate ways to start a fire without matches or lighters. Fire needs three components: heat, air, and fuel. To keep a fire going, all three must be in adequate supply. To build a fire:

1. Collect a pile of tinder on the ground. Dried grass, small twigs, dry bark, shredded newspaper, and tissue paper can all be used as tinder, as they burn easily.

2. Start a spark or flame to ignite the tinder. The following methods can be used if you do not have matches or lighters or wish to conserve what you have.

Magnesium fire starter. Magnesium fire starters are inexpensive, costing around $3 to $10, so you should have one in your emergency kit. Most magnesium fire starters consist of flint, striker, and magnesium fuel. To use, scrape the magnesium block with the striker or knife and make a small pile of magnesium shavings (approximately nickel size) onto a piece of paper or dried leaf. Place your tinder bundle close to the shavings. When you have everything ready, use your knife or striker to scrape the flint side of the magnesium bar in a rapid motion. Aim toward the magnesium shavings so the spark can cause them to flare up. Feed your fire with the tinder next to it.

9-volt battery and steel wool. Thin out the steel wool (fine-grade works best) by pulling on the fibers to spread it out. Place it on your tinder bundle. To start the fire, simply touch the tip of the 9-volt battery to the steel wool and it will instantly ignite. Avoid breathing in the fumes from the burning steel wool. Steel wool will ignite even when wet, so it is a good idea to keep some in your bug out bag (you can always use the rest to scrub your cooking utensils).

Magnifying glass and sunlight. Focus direct sunlight through a magnifying glass toward a bundle of tinder. Keep your hand steady while focusing the sunlight. When you see a glowing spot, gently blow on it to keep it going. If you do not have a magnifying glass, you can use a camera lens, binoculars, or even a pair of reading glasses to focus the sunlight. Place a drop of water on the glass to increase the focus.

Bottled water and sunlight. If you have nothing more than a plastic bottle with water, you can still start a fire on a sunny day. Remove the label from the water bottle. Use your water bottle to focus the sunlight on your tinder. You may have to move it around to find the best spot. When you see the glowing tinder, blow on it to encourage the flame.

NAVIGATION

How to tell how much daylight is left without a watch: Hold your arm out with your hand positioned horizontally between the sun and the horizon. Count the number of times you can stack your hand and/or fingers. Each finger represents 15 minutes, and four fingers will equal 1 hour. If you can stack your hands twice in the space between the sun and the horizon, then you have 2 hours of daylight left. If you can stack your hand once, plus two fingers, then you only have 1 hour and 30 minutes of daylight left. This method can be a lifesaver if you are out in the wilderness without a way to tell time. You can gauge how much daylight you have left so you can return back to base camp in a timely manner.

Learn to navigate without a compass. If you find yourself without a compass while stranded, you can determine direction using the following methods:

SHADOW STICK METHOD

You will need:

straight stick or branch, about 3 feet long

3 to 4 rocks

Directions:

1. If you have a tree branch, remove any secondary branches so you are only left with the main branch. Place the stick or branch on the ground in a flat, clear area as straight as possible. You may have to reinforce it with a few rocks to stand it up straight. Look at the shadow cast by the stick or branch and mark the end of the shadow with a rock. This first point will be west.

2. Wait for 15 minutes. Take another rock and mark the end of the shadow cast by the stick or branch. This will be east. In the Northern Hemisphere, the movement will

be in a clockwise direction; in the Southern Hemisphere, it will be counter-clockwise.

3. Draw a line between the two points. To find north and south, stand with the first mark (west) at your left side, and the second mark (east) at your right side. You will be facing north, and behind you will be south.

ANALOG WRIST WATCH METHOD

If your watch is working properly and the sun is visible, you can find north and south.

Northern Hemisphere: Point the hour hand at the sun. Look at the "12" in your watch. The midpoint between the hour hand and 12 is south.

Southern Hemisphere: Point the watch's 12 toward the sun. The midpoint between 12 and the hour hand is north.

LEARN TO SHARPEN A KNIFE WITH A ROCK

A knife is an essential tool for survival, but using a dull knife can be dangerous. That's because you have to use more force or pressure to cut anything with a dull knife, causing you to potentially lose control and cut yourself. The good news is you can sharpen a knife with a rock. Sandstone, quartz, or granite work well. If you don't know how to identify rocks, find a smooth, flat rock, preferably near a body of water. The water from streams or rivers flows over the rocks and wears them down over time. The ideal stone would have a rough surface on one side and a smooth surface on the other side. Or, you can have two different rocks, one with a coarser grain, the other with a fine, smooth surface.

To sharpen, hold the knife handle with your right hand with the blade facing up. Hold the coarser stone with your left hand. Keeping your fingers a safe distance away, place the flattest part of the stone up against the edge of the blade and make tiny circles with the stone against the blade. Do the same with the other side of the blade.

Next, use the flattest part of the smooth stone and make the same tiny circles against the blade, first on one side, then the other side.

Tip: If you happen to need knife-sharpening while at home, you can also use the unglazed bottom of a coffee mug to sharpen a knife. On a stable surface, turn the mug upside down. Using your dominant hand, hold the knife at about a 30-degree angle against the unglazed bottom of the cup, while holding the mug down with the other hand. Run the blade across, in an upside down "U" motion from left to right, then from right to left. Always keep the blade away from you. In about five or six swipes, the blade will be sharp.

LEARN TO COOK OVER AN OPEN FIRE

Cooking over an open fire is very different from cooking on a stove. Try it in your backyard or at a campground. Some campgrounds have designated fire rings, while others require setting up your own fire ring with large rocks. Don't use rocks from a river bed, as the water inside the cracks may eventually cause the rocks to explode. Make sure your fire is in an open area, away from trees, tents, or any debris that can catch fire.

Requires:

- long-handled utensils, such as tongs, a spatula, and a cast-iron pan
- thick heat-protective gloves or oven mitts
- metal pots or pans (Teflon- or silicon-coated pan may overheat and get damaged from excessive heat)

Start the fire at least 30 minutes to 1 hour before you start cooking to get the coals going. Position your fire a bit to one side of the rocks where you will set your cooking pot. That way, you can move the coals back and forth if you need to adjust the heat. Gather firewood and place your tinder and kindling bundle on top of your firewood. Start your fire, ignite the tinder, and wait for the kindling bundle to burn along with the firewood. As the firewood burns, it will turn black, break up, and glow at its center—this means it has turned into hot coals. When you have several hot coals, move them into the middle of the ring where you will set your pot to cook. The coals are what you actually cook with, not the roaring fire.

You can also cook over the coals with a grill. You can place your pots and pans over the grill, or place foods directly on the grill.

Cook with Cast-Iron Pots

The best cookware to use over an open fire is cast iron because it distributes heat evenly. Once well-seasoned, it becomes a nonstick pan. Cast-iron pans work well over any type of stove. You can even bake with them in the oven. They are very sturdy, yet inexpensive: It costs $10 for a new, unseasoned pan, and $20 for a new, pre-seasoned pan. Seasoning is the process of treating a cast-iron pan with oils so that it develops a nonstick surface. The color of the pan darkens as it becomes more seasoned.

The most inexpensive cast-irons pans can be bought used at thrift stores or garage sales. Don't worry if you see a little rust: As long as the pan does not have pits and the bottom of the pan is level, you can re-season the pan and restore it.

HOW DO YOU SEASON A CAST-IRON PAN?

If you have a new pan, wash and rinse the pan. If you are re-seasoning a pan with some rust in it, scrape off the rust with a stiff brush or steel wool in hot soapy water, then rinse well. Dry it completely with a dish towel. Coat the cleaned pan with vegetable oil or melted vegetable shortening.

Place aluminum foil on the bottom of the oven, as your pan will drip some of the oil.

Place the pan upside down in the oven and heat it to 350°F. Do not leave the hot oven unattended. You may notice some smokiness. After an hour, turn off the heat. Let the pan stay in the oven as it cools. After it cools, you can store it and use as needed.

Repeat the process over a few months until the pan turns black. The process generally takes about three to four cycles of oiling and baking before it turns nonstick.

Do not use soap on your cast-iron pan after the first washing. To clean, use a scrubber and hot water to scrape off dirt. Coat with oil after use.

If you have never used a cast-iron pan, give it a try. You'll save money as you never have to replace them. With proper care, cast-iron pans can last for generations.

LEARN HOW TO MAKE A SURVIVAL SHELTER FROM A TRASH BAG

A large, 45- or 55-gallon construction-grade trash bag can be used to make an emergency survival shelter. It will give you protection from wind, rain, and cold, and is also portable enough to carry around. Large orange- or yellow-colored bags can also help you get spotted by rescuers if you are lost.

To make one, cut a hole on the closed end of the bag; make the hole big enough so you can fit your head through. When you need the shelter, place the bag over your head so that your face is exposed but your head, shoulders, and arms are covered.

Tuck your feet in under you. The trash bag shelter is meant to be a makeshift shelter for temporary emergency use if you find yourself in inclement weather without a tent.

LEARN CPR AND FIRST AID

The Red Cross and American Heart Association offer low-cost CPR and first aid classes. You can find them by searching online and providing your zip code for classes near you. I've worked at various hospitals that offer free community courses for CPR and first aid; check with your local hospital regarding their community outreach programs.

LEARN ABOUT FIRST RESPONDERS

The Federal Emergency Management Agency (FEMA) provides classes so average citizens can be knowledgeable about how to respond in the event of a disaster. These classes are called CERT, which stands for Community Emergency Response Team. These are a series of classes provided in many counties all over the country to train people in disaster preparedness. Here are some available CERT courses:

- Disaster Preparation
- Disaster Response
- Fire Suppression
- First Aid
- Hazardous Materials
- Incident Command
- Search and Rescue

Classes are usually held in a fire station or other community meeting place and are free of charge. You can find out more about CERT programs by visiting http://www.fema.gov/community-emergency-response-teams.

MAKE A POCKET SURVIVAL KIT

There are times when you are unable to carry a full survival kit with you. Make your own pocket survival kit to carry the smallest essentials that you can tuck in your desk, pocket, or purse. You can use a recycled mint tin, such as an Altoids tin, and include items that you'll most likely find useful in an emergency. Some sample contents I have included in mine are:

- antibacterial wipes
- Band-Aids
- cash and coins
- Mylar blanket
- packet of pain reliever
- safety pins
- strike anywhere matches

The contents are entirely up to you. Replenish as you use them up, or replace when your needs change.

Chapter 12

MAKING YOUR OWN

We've spent most of our time discussing ways to prepare with a small budget, but there is one more avenue to preparedness that does not require a large cash outlay. I am talking about acquiring self-sufficiency skills during your free time. It may take a small time investment, but most of the time you can do your research for free in the library or Internet. No one can truly be self-sufficient, but learning even just one skill and becoming proficient at it is very rewarding and will ultimately save you money.

Entire books are devoted to these pursuits. However, I wanted to give you a few "quick start" suggestions.

COOK AND BAKE FROM SCRATCH

Reduce your reliance on store-bought and restaurant foods by learning how to cook and bake from scratch. There are more advantages to homemade cooking besides saving money. It reduces waste and is good for the environment. Many items are healthier choices without all the chemicals and preservatives.

It also spares you from running to the store every time you run out of something.

ARTISAN BREAD

Bread making does not need to be intimidating; it can be very easy. All it takes is a willingness to experiment. Fresh homemade artisan bread is so much better than store-bought bread, and it makes the house smell delicious. Because homemade bread has no preservatives, one thing you will notice is the bread does not last for a week like store-bought, sliced bread. However, because it tastes good, the family generally eats it up a lot more quickly as well.

You will need:

1½ tablespoons granulated yeast (about 1½ packets)

1½ tablespoons sea salt

3 cups lukewarm water, plus more during baking

6½ cups unsifted, unbleached flour

Directions:

1. In a large bowl or plastic container, mix the yeast and salt with the lukewarm water (about 100°F). Stir in the flour, mixing until there are no dry patches. Dough will be quite loose. Cover, but not with an airtight lid. Let dough rise at room temperature 2 to 5 hours.

2. You can either bake or refrigerate the dough at this point. To store, refrigerate it, covered, for as long as 2 weeks. When you are ready to bake, sprinkle a little flour on the dough and cut off a grapefruit-sized piece

with a serrated knife. Turn the dough in your hands to lightly stretch the surface, creating a rounded top and a lumpy bottom. Set the grapefruit-sized dough on a baking sheet and let it rest for 40 minutes. Repeat with the remaining dough or keep the rest refrigerated.

3. Dust the dough with flour once more and make three slashes across the top with a serrated or very sharp knife. Place the baking sheet with the dough into a preheated 450°F oven. Place a broiler pan with 1 cup of water on the bottom rack of the oven, then shut the oven quickly to trap steam. Check after 15 minutes to see if the water has evaporated, and if so, add another cup of water. Keep baking until the bread is well-browned, about 30 minutes. Cool completely before serving.

- This dough can be stored in the refrigerator.
- Makes four 1-pound loaves.

Based on "Artisan Free Form Loaf" from *Artisan Bread in Five Minutes a Day: The Discovery that Revolutionizes Home Baking* by Jeff Hertzberg and Zoe Francois (Thomas Dunne Books, 2007).

MY FAVORITE BREAD MACHINE RECIPE

Using a bread machine saves money and takes the guesswork out of making bread. Sure, there is an initial outlay for buying the bread machine, but if you use it regularly, it will pay for itself very quickly.

Shop around before you buy. New bread machines cost $90 to $150, and nearly new ones are sold on Craigslist for around $15 to $25. Most of the bread machines I saw advertised are either new or had only been used once—most of them still had the original packaging and manuals.

You need measure all ingredients precisely in the bread machine. Read the manual and follow all instructions to the letter.

You will need:

1 cup water	3 cups bread flour
2 tablespoons sugar	½ teaspoon salt
1 envelope packet of yeast	

Directions:

1. Heat the water in the microwave for 40 seconds to warm. Add the warmed water to the bread machine.

2. Add the sugar and mix well.

3. Add the yeast; it will bubble.

4. Add the flour and the salt and mix in.

5. Set the bread machine to a 1.5-pound loaf, medium crust, at the Basic Bread setting. Most bread cycles usually take a little over 3 hours to complete.

6. When ready, remove the bread and serve. This bread stays fresh about 3 days, at the most.

HOMEMADE VANILLA

Vanilla extract is used in a lot of dessert recipes and can be expensive. It is very easy to make vanilla at home for your own use as well as for gifts.

You will need:

4 vanilla beans	glass jar with lid
2 cups vodka	sharp knife

Directions:

1. Using the knife, slice the vanilla beans lengthwise down the middle.

2. Place the vodka in the glass jar. Place the vanilla beans in the vodka, soaking it completely.

3. Leave the mixture in a cool, dark place for 6 months, swirling it once a month. The mixture will turn darker as it ages. You can make larger batches as long as you use the same ratio of 2 vanilla beans per cup of vodka.

HOMEMADE GREEK YOGURT

You will need:

4 cups milk, plus 2 tablespoons to be saved and used later	cooking thermometer (a turkey thermometer works)
2 tablespoons Greek yogurt	spoon
slow cooker	aluminum foil
2 towels	2 bath towels

mesh strainer

large coffee filter or cheesecloth

small pot

container for storing

Directions:

1. Pour the 4 cups of milk into the slow cooker and set on low for 1½ hours. Once the milk reaches 170°F, turn off the heat and let cool for 20 to 40 minutes.

2. Check the temperature after 20 to 40 minutes. The milk should have cooled down to 105°F to 110°F. You will notice a "skin" has formed on top of the milk.

3. Once you reached 105 to 110°F, use a spoon to mix the 2 tablespoons of milk with 2 tablespoons of Greek yogurt. Pour the milk/yogurt mixture down the side of the slow cooker to avoid disturbing the skin that has formed on top of the lukewarm milk.

4. Cover the slow cooker first with aluminum foil, then with the lid. Then cover it with two bath towels to keep it lukewarm. Leave it alone for 8 to 12 hours while it thickens. I checked mine after about 4 hours and the slow cooker had cooled completely, so I turned it on "warm" for about 10 minutes, then turned it off again. I left it alone for the rest of the time.

5. After 8 to 12 hours, you will see that the yogurt has thickened but has some liquid around it. Do not leave it much longer than 12 hours, as the yogurt will get more sour.

6. Line the mesh strainer with the coffee filter (or cheesecloth) and set it over a small pot.

7. Pour the yogurt into the strainer and let it drain for 15 to 20 minutes. About ¾ to 1 cup of liquid will drain into the pot. Some cooks use this liquid for baking.

8. Pour the yogurt into a container and refrigerate before using. It will firm up some more after it has cooled. Save a few tablespoons of yogurt for your next batch.

SWEET TEA

This is a favorite in our household during the summer months. We like plain black tea or orange pekoe, but you can use any type, including herbal tea.

You will need:

8 cups water, divided	pinch of baking soda
6 tea bags	¾ cup sugar

Directions:

1. Boil 2 cups of the water.

2. When the water boils, remove from heat and add your tea bags. Steep for no more than 15 minutes so the tea does not become bitter.

3. After 15 minutes, remove the tea bags and add a pinch of baking soda.

4. Pour the brewed tea into another container and add 6 cups of cool water.

5. Add the sugar and mix well.

6. Refrigerate until cool.

HOMEMADE GRANOLA

Granola can be expensive when store-bought. When you make your own at a much cheaper price, you'll know exactly what ingredients to use based on what you like.

You will need:

2 cups old-fashioned oats

½ cup dried raisins or cranberries 1 cup nuts

1 teaspoon ground cinnamon

¼ teaspoon salt

½ stick butter

¼ cup lightly packed brown sugar

¼ cup honey

1 teaspoon vanilla

baking sheet

aluminum foil

small bowl

medium saucepan

Directions:

1. Preheat the oven to 350°F. Line a baking sheet with aluminum foil. Grease the surface with oil or cooking spray.

2. Mix the oats, raisins or cranberries, nuts, cinnamon, and salt in a small bowl.

3. Combine the butter, sugar, and honey in a medium saucepan over medium heat. Stir until the butter melts and begins to boil. Add the vanilla and stir. Remove from the heat and pour over the oats. Make sure oats get coated well.

4. Transfer the mixture to the baking sheet, spreading it flat in an even layer.

5. Place the sheet in preheated oven and check after 15 minutes. Stir in any edges that are getting too brown. Return to oven and bake another 10 to 15 until top is golden.

6. Remove from heat and let cool. Break into chunks.

DOG BISCUITS

I used to buy dog biscuits at the pet store until I started hearing about pets becoming ill from recalled food. I made dog biscuits by trial and error until I found the right combination for our dog. Bacon grease seems to be the favorite ingredient—save grease when you cook bacon and use it to flavor homemade dog biscuits. If you don't have bacon grease, you may use olive or vegetable oil.

You will need:

3 cups flour

1 egg (or 2 egg whites)

½ cup hot water

½ teaspoon chicken bouillon

¼ cup bacon grease (or olive or vegetable oil)

½ teaspoon salt (optional)

Directions:

1. Preheat the oven to 350°F.

2. Mix all of the ingredients for 3 minutes until the mixture forms a ball. Knead until smooth.

3. Add more water in ½-teaspoon increments if the mixture feels too dry. You should be able to flatten the dough.

4. Use a wine bottle or rolling pin to flatten. When $^1/_{16}$ inch thin, use a cookie cutter or a jar cover to cut into shapes.

5. This recipe will make about 24 to 30 biscuits, depending on the size of the cookie cutter.

6. Grease the baking sheet with bacon grease or vegetable oil. Lay the shapes flat on the baking sheet. Poke each biscuit with a fork before baking.

7. Bake for 25 to 30 minutes.

GARDENING

Learning to grow your own food is a great skill: You'll eat healthier, as well as save some money if you can grow a few herbs, vegetables, and fruits.

Even if you don't have a lot of room, you can learn how to grow food by starting out with a few herbs on a window sill. Although many gardening experts recommend growing them from seed, I recommend that beginners start by procuring starter plants. The easiest way to get started is to pick up a few herb pots at the grocery or garden store. Farmer's markets also sell a good selection of herbs. They are inexpensive and sell for about $3 to $4 a pot. The easiest to grow are mint, oregano, basil, and thyme. Cilantro is useful, but I find it harder to maintain than the rest.

Once your herbs start thriving, transfer them to larger pots. You will enjoy snipping fresh herbs for your own use.

Growing Herbs and Vegetables from "Trash"

This might sound strange, but it actually works. Many plants can re-grow from discarded ends. Avoid waste and start your garden by rescuing vegetables you may otherwise have thrown in the trash bin.

Green onions: I started noticing that green onion roots grow slightly while stored in the refrigerator, so I decided to try an experiment. After using up the green onion stalks, I kept the root parts and left them in water. After 2 to 3 days, the roots started growing and fresh green onion shoots sprouted. I then transferred them to some potting soil and a whole new crop of green onions grew from the roots. My green onion supply lasted for several months until the cold weather came in.

Celery: After my success with green onions, I saved the bottom part of the celery. The white part that usually gets thrown out will actually grow roots if you set it in water. Once roots appear, transfer the growing celery to soil. After about

7 to 10 days, fresh celery leaves will grow upward. Soon after this come fresh celery stalks. The same process also works with other vegetables, such as romaine lettuce and bok choy.

Garlic: Plant intact garlic bulbs in soil. Soon garlic shoots will sprout.

Ginger: Plant part of your unused ginger in soil with the parts that look like "eyes" facing up.

CANNING

My grandmother used to make the best pineapple jam. Every summer, she would set aside a day or two to do her canning, then give away the delicious bounty to friends and relatives. I was young at the time and mostly remember helping to stir the jam as it cooked.

I wish I had learned all the steps involved, as canning is a great skill. Reportedly, home canning has started gaining popularity in the last few years as consumers discover that a small initial investment can lead to substantial savings in the food budget, as well as control over nutritional content.

Canning is also an excellent way to supplement your food storage, which is why we will spend a few minutes discussing the basics.

Equipment

Canning equipment is sold at supermarkets, discount stores, hardware stores, and gourmet kitchen stores; online retailers such as Amazon and eBay also carry them. As for budget sources, I have found canning equipment at thrift stores such as Goodwill, yard sales, and estate sales. If you are going the budget route, here are a few tips:

- Use only "real" canning jars such as those made by Jarden, Mason, or Ball. Do not attempt to use store jars.

- If you reuse canning jars, they must not have any chips or cracks.

- Seals, the flat part of the lid that seals to the jar, cannot be reused.

- Rings, also known as bands that are used to hold the lids in place, can be reused as long as they are not bent, rusty, or mangled.

Another way to save money is to borrow canning equipment or try canning with a knowledgeable friend or relative. Have a canning party and everyone can bring canning jars and ingredients to preserve food.

Water bath canning is the most basic way to preserve high-acid foods, such as strawberries, apples, pickles, and tomato sauce. My grandmother used the water bath canning method to make her pineapple jam.

Pressure canning is the only method used for canning low-acid foods, such as vegetables, meats, or dairy, as low-acid foods require higher temperatures for preservation than a water bath canner provides.

If you are a beginner who is concerned about equipment costs or the space required to store it, the best way to start learning is the water bath method.

WATER BATH CANNING

You will need:

canning jars

large water bath canner with a tight lid

jar lifter

drying rack

seals or "flats"

rings

rubber scraper

clean towels

Directions:

1. Wash the canning jars in hot, soapy water, then rinse well.

2. Use your water bath canner to boil the jars. Boil the jars in the pot (on the rack) for at least 10 minutes. Make sure the jars are completely submerged in water. After boiling, remove them from water using the jar lifter and place them upside down on a towel or drying rack. Alternatively, if you have a dishwasher, run the jars through the sanitizer cycle before you start canning.

3. Sanitize the lids. Simmer water a small pot and place the flats and rings inside. Do not boil, as this may damage the seals. Just keep them in the hot water and

remove using tongs or the lid lifter when you are ready to seal the jars.

4. Start heating your canner as you prepare the food you are planning to can. Place the rack in the bottom of the canner and fill with water. Remember to leave a few inches at the top so you have room for the jars. Heat the water to boiling.

5. Place your canning jars on the counter, over a towel to avoid the risk of slipping. Carefully ladle the prepared food into the jar, leaving the recipe-required head space between the food and the top of the jar.

6. Use a rubber scraper to release any trapped air bubbles and add more food, maintaining head space.

7. Use a clean towel to wipe the rims of the jar; any food particles left on the rim may prevent proper sealing.

8. Place the flats on the jars; tighten the rings with your fingers. The closed jars are ready to be processed in the canner.

9. Using your jar lifter, carefully place the jars into the canner. Do not let the jars touch and bump into each in the water, as they can break. The lids should be at least 1 inch under water, so add more water if needed.

10. Cover the canning pot and heat to boiling. Once it is at a rolling boil, you can start your timer and boil according to the recipe. Add more water if the water level is low, keeping it at a boil.

11. After the prescribed time, remove the jars from the boiling water using your jar lifter. Place the jars on a towel or rack; tip the jar sideways to let any hot water flow off the top.

12. Leave the jars alone for 12 to 24 hours. At this point, the jars will be cooling and sealing; You may hear a pinging noise as the lid seals to the lip of the jar.

13. After at least 12 hours, when the jar cools, check the seals before storing. You can now remove the rings. Using your fingers, press the center of each lid. If the lid moves back and forth, the jar is not sealed. If the jar did not seal properly, store in the refrigerator and use the food within the next week or so.

14. If the lid stays put and you cannot push it up or down, it is properly sealed. The properly sealed jars can be stored in the pantry.

Tips to Ensure Safe, High-Quality Home-Canned Food

- Use fruits or vegetables at the peak of freshness, free of bruises or lesions.
- Can prepared foods as soon as possible.
- Store the jars in a cool, dark place that's between 50°F and 70°F.
- Use your home-canned foods within a year.

IS IT POSSIBLE TO CAN YOUR OWN RECIPES?

Once you have experience following canning and food safety basics, you can start canning your own recipes.

You must still follow the basic rules of canning. List the ingredients in your recipe and search for directions on how to can these ingredients separately. The recipe's total processing time will be based on the ingredient that requires the longest time to be canned safely. Note any special processing instructions for all the ingredients and follow the strictest guidelines so you can be assured that your food is safe to eat.

A few pointers:

- Spices and seasonings take on a more intense flavor in canned recipes, after they have been sitting on your shelf for some time. For example, spaghetti sauce will taste more robust. You may need to dilute the flavor by adding water.

- Stay away from canning foods that are very high in fat, as they can turn rancid more quickly than leaner foods due to the high fat content.

- Avoid using flour or sour cream as a thickener in canning recipes. Instead, add them when you are ready to reheat the canned food.

Source: *The Organic Canner* by Daisy Luther

- Before consuming, inspect the jars and lids. Do not eat if you notice the lid swelling, if the jar has leaked, if you see mold, or if the food does not smell or look good. Discard immediately as contaminated foods can contain harmful bacteria.

- Download the USDA Complete Guide to Home Canning for information and recipes on canning, provided by the US Department of Agriculture (USDA) at http://nchfp.uga.edu/publications/publications_usda.html.

- Check out various books on canning at your local library.

DEHYDRATING/DRYING FOODS

Dehydrated foods take up very little space overall, and it is not difficult to do it yourself as long as you have a food dehydrator.

Food dehydrator prices start at around $15 on eBay or $40 and up on Amazon. Prices vary according to size and features, so do some research on brands before making the purchase.

If you have a garden, you can dehydrate some of the produce from your harvest.

Because most of us do not have our own homestead or farm that provides a supply of fresh vegetables and fruits, the most cost-effective way to make your own dehydrated food is to make it from frozen food.

- 6 cups of frozen spinach will net 1½ cups of dried spinach
- 8 cups of frozen broccoli will net 2 cups of dried broccoli
- 3 cups of frozen green beans will net 1¼ cups of dried green beans
- 6 cups of frozen corn will net 2 cups of dried corn

How to Dehydrate without a Food Dehydrator

If you are not ready to own a food dehydrator but want to try drying foods at home, here are a few options:

Sun drying. If you live in a hot, dry area, you can leave food out in the sun under a screen or cheesecloth. Set a table outside and line it with foil. Place fruit and/or vegetable pieces and cover with a screen or cheesecloth. Make sure the cover is secure as insects or critters may try to get to your food.

Air drying. I have tried air drying herbs with great success.

1. Wash the herbs thoroughly.

2. Without tearing or crushing the leaves, gently dry them with a towel.

3. Lay the herbs on a clean kitchen towel or on a paper towel.

4. Leave the entire thing on a high shelf or another out-of-the-way spot in the house where it can be undisturbed for

a couple of weeks. Another option is to bundle the herbs together with a string and hang the string on a wire rack.

5. Check in 1 week. The rate of drying depends on the humidity level in your area, so your drying time may be quicker if you live in a dry climate.

6. After 3 weeks, the herbs should be thoroughly dry. You know the herb is thoroughly dry when the leaves and stems feel brittle to the touch and are easily crushed with your fingers.

Oven or toaster oven drying. You can use your oven or toaster oven at the lowest setting (around 140°F) to dehydrate fruits and vegetables.

Place sliced fruit or vegetables on a nonstick baking sheet, and place inside the oven. Set the oven or toaster oven at 140°F. Leave the oven door slightly ajar. Drying may take 4 to 12 hours. You will need to turn the baking sheet regularly for even drying.

How to Tell if the Food Is Properly Dehydrated

Keep in mind that home-dehydrated food, unlike freeze-dried or commercially dehydrated food, still contains a trace of moisture. Use your home-dehydrated food within a year of making it. Rotate through it frequently.

FERMENTATION

Fermentation is the process in which a carbohydrate, such as a starch or sugar, is converted into an acid or alcohol. It is the process used to make beer, wine, pickles, and other products.

An easy fermentation project is to make homemade apple cider vinegar. There is a slow way and a fast way to make it yourself. Because this is a beginner's book, let's go over the fast method.

HOMEMADE APPLE CIDER VINEGAR

You will need:

- 1 (16-ounces) bottle organic apple juice
- 1 (16-ounce) bottle all natural, raw, and unfiltered apple cider vinegar, such as Bragg's Raw Unfiltered Apple Cider Vinegar

- wide-mouth containers
- cheesecloths
- rubber bands
- strainer
- sterilized bottles

Directions:

1. Mix equal parts organic apple juice and apple cider vinegar in a wide-mouth container. Cover the container with cheesecloth secured by a rubber band. Store in a dark place and leave it alone to ferment for 3 days to a week or so. If it is warm, the process may be faster.

2. It will ferment and the juice will turn into vinegar. The mixture will form a "mother," which is what you use to

start the next batch of vinegar. The "mother" appears like a spongy pancake. You can smell and taste it to tell whether it is ready. The finished product will have the strong, acidic vinegar smell.

3. When ready, strain the liquid to remove any bits floating around and store in sterilized bottles (similar to vinegar bottles). Cover. Save the "mother" for future batches of vinegar so you will have a never-ending supply. (See step 5 for instructions.) Fill the bottle to the brim completely before covering to stop the fermentation process. Use within a few months. Once you open the bottle, store it in the fridge. Another way to completely stop the fermentation process is by pasteurizing the vinegar.

4. If you prefer a mellower flavor, let the finished vinegar sit for a month or so before using.

5. To make future batches of vinegar, transfer the mother to a wide-mouth glass container. Add a bottle of wine. Cover with a cheesecloth secured by a rubberband and leave undisturbed in a cool, dark space. Check it every week, adding more wine if needed. Taste the vinegar; if you like it, it is time to pasteurize and bottle it.

PASTEURIZED VINEGAR

Vinegar should be pasteurized to slow down the growth of acid-producing bacteria, avoid spoilage, and last longer on the shelf. If you wish to pasteurize the vinegar, strain out the mother first. Heat the vinegar to 170°F for 10 minutes. Use a food thermometer to check the temperature. The easiest way to do this is to heat it in a slow cooker and maintain the temperature for 10 minutes. Store in a sterilized bottle. Pasteurized vinegar will last longer on the shelf, but it will not form a "mother."

CANDLE MAKING

Candle making is a useful skill, since candles are great backup light sources. Even if a disaster never happens, candles are very popular home accessories and gift items. Here is an easy way to get started.

MASON JAR CANDLES

Mason jars are sold at discount stores, such as Walmart or Target, and can also be bought at Goodwill or Salvation Army. I use mason jars, but you can easily use whatever you have on hand. Remember, the rule of thumb is to use twice the amount of wax flakes to the container. For example, if you are using an 8-ounce container (or 1 cup), use 16 ounces (2 cups) of wax flakes.

You will need:

mason jar	large measuring cup
pre-waxed candle wicks	pot
2 skewers	water
Scotch tape	oven mitts
wax flakes of your choice (I use soy wax flakes)	10 to 12 drops essential oils (eucalyptus or lavender are good choices)

Directions:

1. Wash and dry your jar.

2. Place the metal part of the wick flat in the middle of the jar.

3. Tape the two skewers together with the wick suspended in the middle of the two skewers to keep the wick upright.

4. Measure enough wax flakes for your jar. If you are using the 8-ounce mason jar, measure 16 ounces of wax flakes. Keep the wax flakes in the large measuring cup.

5. Fill the pot halfway with water.

6. Place the measuring cup containing your wax flakes in the pot. Make sure the water will not spill out into the wax once it starts to boil.

7. Reduce heat to medium and wait for the wax to melt, stirring occasionally with a spoon.

8. Remove from heat once the wax has completely melted. Use oven mitts, as the cup and oil will be very hot.

9. Add 10 to 12 drops of essential oil to the wax and stir.

10. Pour the wax into the Mason jar.

11. Leave the candle alone to cool and solidify for about 4 hours.

12. Trim the wick, leaving about ½ inch in the candle. Your candle is ready for use.

SOAP MAKING

Many people are intimidated by soap making because it involves the use of lye, a caustic material. However there is a way to become comfortable with soap making by initially using a melt-and-pour soap base. Using a melt-and-pour soap base is similar to using a cake mix to bake a cake: All the ingredients were pre-mixed for you, but you gain the experience and confidence to make it yourself. There is a wide variety of melt-and-pour soap bases available, from cocoa butter and honey to goat's milk.

HOMEMADE SOAP

You will need:

molds (use recycled containers, such as frozen juice cans, muffin pans, bread pan, etc.)

olive oil

melt-and-pour soap base of your choice

large, heat-resistant glass measuring cup

oven mitts

essential oils, such as lavender, lemon, orange, or eucalyptus

spoon

oatmeal, dried rose petals, or lavender buds

rubbing alcohol in a spritzer bottle

plastic cling wrap

Directions:

1. Prepare your molds by spraying or rubbing a small amount of olive oil to the surfaces and wiping off any excess.

2. Cut the soap base into chunky pieces. Place them in the glass measuring cup.

3. Heat the cup with the soap base chunks in the microwave at 30-second intervals until the soap is completely melted. The cup and liquefied soap will be extremely hot, so use oven mitts to remove it from the microwave and keep out of reach of children. Once the soap appears to be a smooth liquid, add your essential oils and oatmeal (if using) to scent your soap. Mix with a spoon to distribute evenly.

4. Pour the melted soap into the molds.

5. If you are adding dried rose or lavender petals, fill the mold halfway with the melted soap and add the petals. Leave it alone for 10 to 15 minutes to set, then add more soap.

6. Once all the molds are filled, spritz the soap-filled molds with rubbing alcohol to get rid of any bubbles.

7. Allow the soap to cool and harden for about 2 hours.

8. Once the soap has cooled, wrap individually in plastic cling wrap and store.

Once you have gone through this process a few times, you may feel ready to make your own soaps in the traditional manner, with lye. Check out instructional books from the library or research tutorials on basic soap making online.

AUTO MAINTENANCE

When I was growing up, I watched my dad do his own auto maintenance: oil and filter changes, simple tune-ups, or even just troubleshooting before he took it to see an auto mechanic. I know he saved a lot of money over the years by doing his own basic car maintenance.

When times are tough, many drivers choose to hang on to their cars longer instead of trading them in for a new car. Knowing how to maintain your car will help you do necessary upkeep to help your car last longer, as well as identify problems before they get worse. It is also a great skill in an emergency if your car suddenly breaks down.

If you are interested in auto maintenance or repair, start spending time with car buffs who like to tinker with cars. There are also many resources online: hundreds of videos on YouTube show DIY tips and detailed instructions on how to address specific issues. You can also take adult education classes at your local high school or community college.

BASIC HOME MAINTENANCE

Do you call a handyman every time something at home needs fixing? It would be really advantageous to be able to do certain repairs yourself, such as replacing a toilet, installing a faucet, repairing drywall, insulating a room, etc. If you have an interest in doing basic home repair, there are a few ways to learn:

- Contact a Home Depot or Lowe's in your area for available classes. These workshops are free and are usually held on weekends. Local hardware stores may also offer free training.

- Volunteer with Habitat for Humanity. Even if you have never picked up a hammer in your life, you'll soon be a pro with hands-on training and more experienced volunteers to show you the ropes.

- Help a friend. If you have friends or relatives who are handy around the house, offer to help out on one of their projects. You'll learn a lot by watching and doing.

- Check out tutorials on the Internet. Several stations, such as the DIY Network and HGTV, show basic home maintenance videos, and episodes of *This Old House* are readily available online. YouTube is also a good source.

Some tasks, such as electrical and plumbing repairs, may require more extensive training—be realistic about how much you can accomplish on your own. If you are a beginner without the right tools or skills, go slowly and don't jump into something that is too complex.

SEWING

In the old days, before clothes and home furnishings were mass produced, sewing was practiced in nearly every household. These days, we no longer have to make our own clothes, curtains, pillows, or blankets, but still occasionally need to alter or repair clothes. During hard times, knowing how to make clothing and other items would be highly useful. You may even pick up a side gig to earn extra money.

Why not take up a new hobby and learn to sew? The last time I had a pair of pants hemmed, I paid $15 for one pair. I had other pairs that needed hemming, so I decided to try doing it myself. I do not own a sewing machine, so I had to do it by hand. My mom had taught me basic stitches, but I did not feel confident enough to make a professional-looking hem. My first attempt at hemming a pair of pants had an undesirable result. But I was not ready to give up. So I turned to YouTube and watched a few videos that looked simple enough. After carefully following the steps in the video, I found success. My hemmed pants looked professionally done. I have not had to pay to have my hems adjusted since.

To get started, assemble your basic sewing kit:

- storage container (You can use a recycled cookie or biscuit tin, plastic storage box with lid, or even a shoe box.)
- pin cushion with straight pins
- assortment of sewing needles
- assortment of thread in various colors
- fabric scissors
- tape measure

You can also purchase a standard sewing kit at Walmart, Target, or Amazon.

If you have relatives or friends who know how to sew, have them show you some basic stitches. The best way to learn how to sew, crochet, or knit is to watch and learn. Watch a few videos online and try it out. You can also sign up for free classes at craft and hobby stores, sewing or quilting guilds, etc.

READY FOR ANYTHING

Being short on funds should not stop you from being prepared. With a little creativity and a lot of comparison shopping, you can make do with basic ingredients and acquire some skills so you too can be ready for emergencies. With that readiness comes peace of mind. I wish you the best in your preparedness journey.

INDEX

ACKNOWLEDGMENTS

To my editor, Renee Rutledge, thank you for keeping me on track and for all your guidance throughout the process of writing this book. To acquisitions editor, Keith Riegert, for your continued support. I am grateful to the entire team at Ulysses Press for all your assistance in producing my book.

To the writers at the Professional Prepared Bloggers Association, I appreciate the kind encouragement and rapport. Special thanks to Gaye Levy (BackdoorSurvival.com) and Lisa Bedford (TheSurvivalMom.com): We've never met in person, but I have found your advice invaluable.

To all my readers at ApartmentPrepper.com, thank you for supporting my work; you are the reason I keep writing.

To my family, thank you for putting up with all my craziness and for being my test subjects during the writing of the book. You have kept me going and stood by my side through all the ups and downs.

ABOUT THE AUTHOR

Bernie Carr became fascinated with survival techniques and self-sufficiency as a child, hearing stories of her father's adventures in the wilds of Southeast Asia as a land surveyor and avid outdoorsman. As an adult, she developed an interest in emergency preparedness and self-reliance, having survived the 1994 Northridge earthquake in California, the 1992 Los Angeles riots, and the evacuation of her home during the 1993 Southern California wildfires. She relocated to Houston, Texas, in an effort to avoid more natural disasters only to arrive in time to encounter the fury of Hurricane Ike in 2008.

Bernie has a bachelor of science degree from the University of Southern California and has worked as a technical writer in various fields, such as personal finance, insurance, and health care. She is the creator of *Apartment Prepper* (ApartmentPrepper.com), a popular website about preparedness while living in small spaces. She has written two other books, *The Prepper's Pocket Guide* and *Jake and Miller's Big Adventure*. Bernie resides in Texas with her family.